THE HARRIS HAWK

Dedication

This book is dedicated to my mother and father, who
have always encouraged me to fulfil my ambitions.

THE HARRIS HAWK

MANAGEMENT, TRAINING AND HUNTING

LEE WILLIAM HARRIS

Quiller

First published in the UK in 2001
by Swan Hill Press, an imprint of Quiller Publishing Ltd

Reprinted 2003, 2005
Reprinted with updated appendices under the Quiller imprint 2010

British Library Cataloguing-in-Publication Data
   A catalogue record for this book
   is available from the British Library

ISBN 978 1 84037 146 8

Printed in China

Quiller

An imprint of Quiller Publishing Ltd
Wykey House, Wykey, Shrewsbury, SY4 1JA
Tel: 01939 261616 Fax: 01939 261606
E-mail: info@quillerbooks.com
Website: www.countrybooksdirect.com

PREFACE

There is little more pleasing than to write a book on a subject which is dear to my heart and on a species which I have been privileged and proud to partner over many seasons.

Before I could initially put pen to paper however, I needed to enter upon some intense research. Although the Harris hawk now commonly graces the inners of many falconers' weatherings, and although I like to think I have built up a working rapport with the species it was remarkable to discover just how little knowledge I actually had. I was, so I thought, fully congnisant of their distribution, hunting techniques and the different wing spans and torso sizes of the different subspecies. I was, again so I thought, observant of their many traits. But to sit down and study the species so intensely made me aware of numerous things which, I am ashamed to say, I did not know, once again highlighting the fact that my knowledge was extremely limited and even stagnant.

In the UK I think we take species such as the kestrel for granted, as it is now so extensive. This, I believe, is probably also true of the Harris hawk. Although not indigenous to Britain, successful captive breeding programmes throughout the country have made this bird both available and affordable to all bar a few of today's practising falconers. Its popularity throughout the UK almost gives one the feeling that it is indigenous.

I have probably learnt only a fraction of what there is to know about this fascinating hawk in its wild state, but that is far more then I previously knew and I am determined that this new-found knowledge will never leave me.

Finally, but to me most importantly, if this book has taught me anything, it is that I shall never again look at our own indigenous birds and take for granted their ability to hunt and survive, as I have been indelibly reminded just how fascinating and hard the natural world is for birds of prey; their quest for survival is one of a constant battle.

NOTE: Throughout this book, falconers are referred to in the masculine gender. This of course, should be taken to mean both men and women where appropriate.

Lee William Harris

ACKNOWLEDGEMENTS

Once again I find myself thanking both friends and associates who have given me their time, knowledge and expertise. To them all I am eternally grateful.

In particular I should like to thank Neil Gwilt of Reflections Photography, Paul Harris, Nigel Pitts, Paul Beecroft, Jim Moss of Crown Falconry for supplying the rubber-finished bow perch featured throughout and Philip Stapelberg, BVSc (Pret), MRCVS. I also thank Julia Wright for the line drawings and for her time spent reading the manuscript. A very special thank you goes to my dear friend Chris Windsor, who under restricted circumstances went out of his way to help me gather information regarding the earliest Harris hawks to enter the UK. I also thank him for his colour illustrations. I should like to express my gratitude to the John James Audobon society in the USA for all their help, guidance and e-mails.

Finally I thank Andrew Reid and his staff at the Belmont Polo Centre, Mill Hill, London, for the use of his estate and horses.

CONTENTS

On this note, dear friends, I would like to leave you with a few wise words which were told to me many years ago by an ageing falconer: 'Falconry is the greatest and most demanding field sport in the world. Respect its values and it cannot fail to grow stronger.'

I hope you enjoy reading this book; writing it was no less than exhilarating.

BASIC KNOWLEDGE

Harris hawks and man

Birds of prey, the art of falconry – truly a fascinating combination. Although I enjoy many field pursuits, falconry is the one for which my passion runs deepest. The intense process of manning, training and hunting with a raptor is now something which I could not live without. Bonding with such beauty, stealth, power and majesty gives me a feeling of inexplicable contentment.

Not only do I take great pleasure from owning and tending to my birds, I feel honoured and extremely lucky that these days I earn my living from those that I keep and the accessories that falconers require. Through conducting both flying displays and educational talks, I have been able to meet numerous members of the public and, in my own small way I have been able to educate many as to the reasons why ordinary people like myself keep these majestic predators. I never become tired of explaining how the birds are housed, managed, trained and maintained. Raptors and owls fascinate the public and it is other people's interest which to a degree keeps my own interest alive.

It is extremely encouraging to see our sport steadily gaining the attention of more new people each year. Never before have we here at the Eagle-Owl School of Falconry received so many enquiries from those wishing to attend one of our falconry courses. This increase in interest is welcome, as not only does it give falconry a freshness, which is something that all sports require, but it maximises growth and strength, especially when there are so many members of the public against all field sports.

Here at the Eagle-Owl School Of Falconry, our course bookings have been on the increase each year for the last five years. This is no doubt due to an increase in the numbers of books and videos on the market, in the numbers of clubs and in the amount of television and media exposure. Game fairs and country shows now appear empty and bleak if there is not a bird of prey flying display team, as it is probably the number one event within the arena throughout the day.

But although the last five years or so have seen a dramatic increase in interest, man has for centuries been enchanted with birds of prey. They have been the inspiration for both artists and poets, whilst cultures around the world have given them god-like status, as they embody freedom and power. Countries portray them in symbols on their national flags and coats of arms. It is not surprising, therefore, that humans have developed such a special relationship with these magnificent rulers of the skies (see colour plates a, b and c).

Described as the oldest sport in the world, falconry has notable traditions and strong values which are firmly embedded in the approach of the modern participant. It is not an easy sport, nor one which the participant ever truly masters as it requires many skills, all of which calls for great dexterity. One must be proficient in leathercraft, field management, bird management, quarry recognition, dietary values and basic health care, to name but a few.

In years gone by, the flying of tame falcons was taken extremely seriously as it was a means of securing the food necessary for human survival. It is believed that falconry was probably one of the first methods of hunting ever adopted by man. It started in China in approximately 2000 BC, and thrived in many places around the globe. It was introduced into Europe by the Romans, and the Dutch became the continent's premier falconers. England first saw the sport evolve during the second half of the ninth century AD, and it remained popular up until the seventeenth century, when folk started to take their pleasure from shooting birds on the wing, regarding raptors as little more than vermin.

Monarchs such as Henry VIII, Edward III, Alfred the Great, Ethelbert II and Mary Queen of Scots were all keen participants and frequently carried out their sport from horseback. Only the most senior nobles were permitted to fly such birds as the saker falcon and gyr falcon, as these marked one's importance and standing within society. A servant would therefore fly a lesser-regarded bird such as the kestrel. Trained hawks and falcons were highly prized and regarded as assets. Birds would be offered as gifts between countries and accepted as payment of outstanding fines and rent.

Although the ancient art of falconry was not consistently practised in many countries, often high in popularity for a time, then out of fashion, people in West Africa, the Middle East and the Orient have all been lovers of the sport and it has never lost its appeal in these areas.

It is held in truly high regard in the Gulf region, commanding the greatest levels of respect. The people there have a genuine commitment to falconry and participants must practise it correctly, according to Islamic customs.

The traditions of the sport have hardly changed from the earliest days. It remains physically and mentally demanding, time-consuming and fraught with difficulties. But if one is prepared to step onto the first rung of the ladder in a quest to master this fine art then one will receive payment back in full, with memorable flights and kills, and an overwhelming feeling of achievement.

Although there are 290 species of raptor throughout the world and another 160 species of owl, the modern falconer has a particularly soft spot for the Harris hawk and it is now the number one flown bird in the UK and possibly throughout Europe. It has a pleasant nature and loves to be in the company of the falconer. The eyass freshly taken from her parents will soon calm down and readily accept her new surroundings. She will not require long, intense manning sessions like other hawks, but will enjoy the occasional night indoors in front of the television, mixing with the family. The Harris will bring the novice compatibility, an easygoing temperament and the competence to fly a wide range of quarry. She will succumb to the manning and training process at a prolific rate provided she is not held back, and will be eager to make her first kill. She will not, however, as some suggest, be an easy bird to train; very little to do with falconry could be regarded as easy. Any bird will be *easier* to those with many seasons behind them. But the novice must realise that the Harris can be stubborn and annoying, just like any other hawk, and nothing must be taken for granted.

The wide variety of quarry which the Harris hawk is capable of taking is encouraging, ranging from sparrows to cock pheasants to hares. They should not be allowed to specialise in any particular species, but encouraged to fly an array of prey; they have taken well over fifty different species. So your day's hawking may be productive even when rabbits are scarce, whereas if your bird is a rabbit specialist then you will have a miserable day if rabbits are nowhere to be seen. How much better to have a spontaneous flight on a pheasant, woodcock or moorhen making an otherwise dull day exciting.

For a Harris hawk fan such as myself, it is all too easy to get carried away and glamorise this bird a little more than it might deserve, as it does have one major fault – a natural dislike of dogs. Because of this, those who want to work a dog may find themselves going through several birds until one is found with the temperament required. With this in mind, it is wise to show the eyass a dog within days of her being brought home from the breeder, and hope that the open wings and mouth, high crest, bating and possible screaming are soon overcome, and that the bird will realise that she is just being silly and the dog is not a threat but an ally. Even if she does come to accept your dog, however, and this is not impossible, there is no guarantee that she will welcome the presence of those belonging to other falconers, which again is a potential problem.

Personally, I feel incomplete if I am not hawking with a competent dog. A little male I once flew had everything that one could expect; he was brave and fast, followed on brilliantly and knew how to hunt. His only problem was he would not tolerate a dog of any kind. From an early age he more or less lived with my German short-haired pointer, but he positively refused to work over her. If we were out hunting even the sight of a dog in the distance could ruin my day. Unfortunately those that will not fly over a dog can never be trained to do so. It is a mental problem and the falconer who is purchasing an eyass of the year can do little more than keep his fingers crossed and hope.

Another potential problem not with the bird, but more with the novice falconer, is a reluctance to let the bird progress at the pace best suited to her. She will often be held back, and kept on the creance far longer than is necessary. This is a big mistake as Harrises are intelligent and quick to learn. If they are constantly denied the opportunity to fly free and achieve fitness they will become both bored and frustrated, which could be demonstrated in screaming and showing none of the customary easygoing traits. Most falconers hate the restriction of the creance and will want to dispense with it as quickly as possible. Flying a bird for too long on the creance will annoy her, even if it does not bother you. Assess your bird's performance thoroughly during each training session and move to the next stage immediately she is ready.

Once your bird is flying free and fit, you can enjoy the added stimulation of flying two Harrises together at the same quarry. This is known as a cast and is rather unique to this species. Flying a cast is certainly exciting, and it is natural in the wild. And it does not result in both birds violently tearing the flesh from the quarry. It is ideal if a smaller male is flown at hare. Should he get thrown off, there is the reassurance of knowing that the larger female is just behind, ready to give a helping foot.

The one question which students ask me more than any other, once they have decided to fly a Harris hawk, is whether they should purchase a male or a female. This is a personal choice, and there is no definite answer. What you should do however, is take into account the land and quarry which is on offer to you. If, for example, the quarry is mainly rabbit, squirrel and hare, then the female will be more suitable. If it is mainly rabbit and moorhen then you may find the male more favourable. Only you can decide.

Personally, I prefer males. They are nimble on the turn, faster to leave the fist, speedier in flight and probably have the preferred temperament. They also suit the majority of land over which I have permission to fly. Unfortunately, they will generally lose the struggle on larger ground quarry and only the foolish would use a male to fly squirrel; in fact, very few falconers will intentionally fly even the larger females at squirrel, as a bird can sustain nasty wounds from such quarry. Over many years I have had the pleasure of working both males and females, all with different temperaments, ability and interest. The vast majority, it has to be said, have been more than skilful, and have shown a genuine hunger for work, whilst a minority have frustrated me to the point of wanting to give in. Hawking is extremely demanding, and there is no room for anything other than a hawk in tip-top condition that shows a degree of natural ability. The falconer then has the duty of bringing out the best in the bird by using his knowledge and experience.

Harris hawks are not as fast as goshawks, nor are they as brave and gutsy as redtails, which for me reduces the excitement. But neither of these birds is best suited to the beginner, certainly not the goshawk. Goshawks are powerful, highly strung and prone to fitting. They have a complicated metabolism and suffer from a low blood-sugar level. It is therefore imperative that the falconer is precise and extremely competent at controlling the hawk's weight, for if she drops below her correct flying weight, or is taken there too abruptly, it can cause her to fit and possibly die.

The redtail is a hawk of immense power. Its temperament is very different from that of the easygoing Harris. Redtails may be suitable for the more mature student who has attended a falconry course and had extensive hands-on experience with such a bird, but for the juvenile, this bird will prove a little too big and powerful.

For the beginner starting off in a sport of such high demands as falconry, the Harris eyass will make life far easier than other species, and any novice must surely want to make life as easy as possible. There have been beginners who have gone straight to the goshawk because of its reputation. The birds bought by these people have been little more than wasted and it is often not long before they realise that they have made a terrible mistake and buy a Harris hawk as soon as possible. Those with little or no experience are well advised to leave any accipiter alone, at least until they have a good few successful seasons behind them.

For me, falconry is about relaxing and enjoying the day, but quality of flight is of vital importance, and it is something the Harris hawk will show time and time again. I do not get my pleasure from the volume of kills in a season; if I did I would purchase a twelve-bore rifle and take up shooting. In its wild state a predator will not kill just for the sake of it. It will hunt to survive and to feed its young, not for any other reason. Nothing sickens me more then to hear so-called falconers boasting about the number of kills their birds have made. Admittedly, it is pleasing and one deserves to be proud when one's bird makes a kill, but to ask a bird to kill unnecessarily just to add another head to the tally is, in my opinion, not what falconry is about. History tells us that man tamed and trained raptors as a means of putting food onto the table. This, I believe, should always be borne in mind. Quality of flight ought to be far more pleasing to the falconer than quantity of kills.

In the UK there is currently no compulsory apprenticeship scheme in operation for falconers and anybody is allowed to own a bird of prey. As a result, we here at Eagle-Owl Falconry are often offered birds such as barn owls and kestrels. Generally they are out of condition, as the owners have not even the basic knowledge to feed them a healthy diet. For this reason alone I cringe at the thought of birds of prey and owls being so easily obtainable. The blame must ultimately fall on the sellers. To offer for sale birds such as these to people with no experience or training in basic bird management and husbandry is extremely immoral; it is the bird which suffers. No reputable breeder would sell any of his birds to such buyers, as they have far more respect for the young which they have so painstakingly reared.

In the USA, things are a little different. Harris hawks are only available to general- and master-level falconers. The apprentice must fly and learn about falconry for two seasons before being legally entitled to possess a bird. This, I feel, gives beginners excellent knowledge and the platform to be worthwhile participants.

Hunting with a Harris hawk is a relaxing style of falconry, with none of the worries associated with goshawks. With this in mind, there are many experienced falconers who jeer at these birds, calling them crows and generally having nothing positive to say about them. But in my opinion, Harris hawks have brought many falconers happiness and have filled a large gap for those who enjoy this almost laid-back style of hawking. I believe the falconer who has spent hour upon hour getting his Harris hawk fit and hunting deserves just the same level of respect as the falconer who has achieved the same result with a goshawk.

Many falconers find that they have all they want in a Harris hawk and feel that changing to another species will involve a search which could well end in disappointment. This is a fair comment, but for every fit, well-trained Harris there will be another which does not do the species any justice. Commitment from the falconer day in and day out is therefore imperative for success, whether with this species or any other. There is no such thing as a weekender's bird.

In summary, the Harris hawk gives solid, consistent and methodical hawking, she will have a more forgiving temperament than any other hawk and she will suit those who have limited flying time during the week. One must always choose a bird to suit one's lifestyle, and not the other way around. The Harris is, in my opinion, the ideal bird with which the beginner should begin his falconry career, and if after twenty or thirty years he is still flying this species, after experimenting with others, then he may agree that it is a bird which is a pleasure to train and fly, a faithful partner and a bird with outstanding ability.

Harris hawks in the wild

From a true falconer's point of view, there is little more engaging than to watch a wild raptor going about her daily life. One particularly fascinating sight is a falcon soaring into the clouds, embodying the ultimate in freedom, co-ordination and skill. Although this is more readily seen in captive-bred birds, every now and again the dedicated birder or the fortunate passer-by may be in luck and stumble upon a wild raptor exquisitely enjoying another meticulous flight.

Many years ago, work took me to Deptford in south-east London.

Driving along a congested road, I spotted two kestrels effortlessly flying amongst the rotating thermals which this splendid day had produced. I stopped the car to take a closer look; like all birders, my binoculars were always to hand. It was apparent that the kestrels were nesting on a large water tank, surrounded by enormous, ageing trees, which helped these little falcons achieve lift. The way in which they gained height was effortless, their wings rarely beating, just expanded and relaxed. Sights like these are not very common, so to see it was a rare pleasure, and one that will remain with me always.

If we look hard enough, we can see our indigenous wild raptors going about their business. Kites, buzzards, falcons, eagles and owls are all around us, and it is often a case of being in the right place and taking the time and having the patience to look. Unfortunately, however, we will never see a true wild Harris hawk gracing our skies. For this we would have to travel 5000 miles to Arizona, USA, as this is home to *Parabuteo unicinctus*, the Harris hawk.

The Harris hawk is a bird of upland desert, semi-desert and sparse woodland territory. It will be seen in its natural state throughout south-western America – Arizona, Texas and south-eastern California – and into Mexico, Argentina and central Chile, where it flourishes.

However, it has not always been this way. To provide hydroelectric power and irrigation water, the American government decided to construct the Hoover dam during the 1930s, and then the Glen Canyon dam during the 1950s. These two constructions meant massive building work on the Colorado River, which left extensive wildlife and scenery destruction. Due to loss of habitat and scarcity of food, Harris hawk numbers dwindled to an all-time worrying low, almost to the point of extinction.

Fortunately, over many years, it was reintroduced by dedicated naturalists to its former lower Colorado range near the Imperial Valley, where it slowly regained its numbers. This beautiful hawk can once again be seen hunting within the valley or perched upon cactus plants in the nearby Anza-Borrego Desert.

Hawks tend to be reasonably large birds and their vantage points are usually in relatively open sites, where they can quite easily be spotted by the birder, providing one is aware of what to look for and where to look. The redtailed hawk as it is called in the USA (buzzard in the UK) is the species most frequently seen throughout America. It is a gutsy bird and easily recognised. It is larger and more powerful than the Harris, and has a completely contrasting coloration. The redtail will freely live alongside man and can be seen on residential roof-tops, window ledges and even basketball nets in gardens.

The Harris hawk (or bay-winged hawk as it is sometimes called in the USA) is more elusive, and Phoenix, Arizona, offers the birdwatcher the best opportunity of spotting it, whether it be on the soar or perched upon

(1) Distribution map

telegraph poles along a highway. In their wild state, Harrises are gregarious and become quite tame, especially the young, and one can get very close to these birds if one approaches with care.

Because Harris hawks are naturally from hotter climates, they are not best suited to countries which have extended cold periods. In the wild, a family of Harrises can huddle together and keep warm should the weather turn, something which they cannot do in captivity unless two birds are in one chamber, for the purposes of breeding perhaps. For falconers in the UK and Europe this means precautionary measures are necessary and special care must be taken when designing the living quarters. In particular, Harris hawks suffer from frostbite and blain.

Frostbite results in wet blisters appearing on the tips of the wings, which eventually go gangrenous and are lost. It can also deaden a hawk's toe, causing it to discolour and, again, to be lost. Many falconers take precautions against frostbite by putting a thermostatically controlled heater in the weathering, positioned above the bird's perching area. If it is set a little higher than the frost setting, one can be confident that the inside will never fall to a worrying temperature. One can also design a heavy-duty sheet (see page 34) which is fixed to the front to the weathering and pulled down overnight to help keep the inside as warm as possible.

Blain, which is inflamed sores and blisters, causes painful swelling, itching and irritation. If a bird is allowed inside her weathering while wet and left overnight she is at high risk of catching this nasty complaint. Any wet bird should be brought indoors and allowed to dry off completely; this will also stop her from catching a chill and reduce the risk of any unnecessary illness. Both blain and frostbite can be prevented, and as any avian vet will tell you, prevention is far better than cure.

If one has a good-sized weathering, it is beneficial to allow the bird freedom of flight. She will then naturally be high off the frosty ground, which will eliminate frostbite. A hawk should however, be fully trained and responsive to the fist before one can allow this so that the falconer can walk into the enclosure and take up his charge with a small offering of food upon the glove. If one has to chase a bird around within such a small area, then there is a very good chance of feather damage or even broken bones. A juvenile Harris has extremely fragile bones, which are easily damaged.

In their wild state Harris hawks will be found gathered in groups, with the older birds co-operating in the raising of the year's young, helping the juveniles to develop pack-hunting skills. This is a vital learning curve for the young immature bird, which requires intense training in the methods of capturing wild quarry. Like all predators, the more experienced warriors will often only injure the prey, letting the inexperienced youngsters finish off the kill. This maintains their enthusiasm and aids in the learning process.

Teamwork is the key to the Harris's success. In the USA they have been compared to lions and wolves, as the communal traits of these predators are in complete contrast to the solitary lifestyles of redtails and other raptors.

The Harris hawk has developed many strategies in a bid to flush, attack and kill prey. A common method is for a group of up to six birds to gather on various vantage points before taking to the wing in search of potential targets. When a target is located, each hawk in turn pounces upon it until it is dead. Another method is for a group to send in one bird at a time to flush out a target from under a bush whilst the others surround the area and swoop in individually for the kill. A third is for the hawks to dive in relay fashion, as many as twenty times, until the prey is caught and killed. Whatever method is used, the whole group eventually shares the meal, in the same way as a pride of lions.

It is also a competent solo bird; it is not totally dependent on hunting in the security of a group. A single-flown captive-bred bird which is well trained and fit, will be quick to kill and meticulous in flight. It will fly in a variety of styles, including soaring and stopping, attack via the fist and following on. A bird which is taught to follow on will not only achieve fitness much sooner, it will also have a better view of potential quarry. Following on involves the bird flying to a tree, taking up a vantage point and waiting. As the falconer walks across the country the hawk will follow him, intensely looking at what he is doing. He may be bashing bushes in an attempt to flush quarry for the bird, which should be high overhead and in a good branch position, as this gives her a natural rush of speed should a rabbit bolt. Many experienced falconers, however, will not allow a juvenile bird to follow on in her first season, as this gives her too much freedom, which may lead to self-hunting – and a self-hunting bird is a liability. Remember, a hawk can see quarry a very long way away, especially from the top of a tall tree, and this can result in the falconer spending a lot of time tracking his bird down. Allowing her to chase via the fist only will help to reduce the risk of self-hunting, at least until her second season when she has learnt her trade and has matured mentally. Personally, I prefer to use shortwings and broadwings solely from the fist as I believe this style is far more exciting and produces a more eye-catching flight.

In their wild state, Harris hawks will feed on a multitude of prey. Although birds, which are often caught in flight, play a major role, small mammals, reptiles, rats, mice, rattlesnakes, quails, spiny lizards, jack-rabbits, desert toads, desert cottontails, ground squirrels and insects are the norm. It is also believed that carrion is eaten, especially when prey is in short supply. The captive-bred Harris also has the potential to fly a variety of quarry, including squirrels, rats, rabbits, hares, ducks, moorhens, pheasants and various other birds. It is a versatile bird which should be shown a variety of game and a variety of scenery, as it will excel in woodland as well as in open and hedgerow areas. In their immature years falconers will benefit from letting their birds chase whatever they wish.

Their curiosity is so intense that they will catch a leaf blowing in the wind for instance. They will soon come to learn that this does not provide a meal but it will help to sharpen their reactions and satisfy their almost childish inquisitive nature.

In the wild, Harris hawks are intensely resentful of other species and are particularly territorial. If threatened, the pack will waste no time in ganging together, wings open to appear bigger and vocal chords screaming, in an attempt to scare off the intruder, although rarely will this prove successful against a hungry bobcat or coyote. Even though it is a large and powerful hawk, the wild Harris has its own share of predators and must always be on its guard. Apart from the bobcat and coyote, which steal the eggs or kill the chicks in the nest if it is built low enough and accessible enough to the ground, other enemies are ravens and the great horned owl. The coyote, however, is the main desert opponent and it seems that the Harris's intense hatred of this canine competitor is transferred into those birds which have been captive-bred, as their dislike of dogs is easily recognised.

Biological facts

Birds of prey and owls are amongst the most spectacular and exquisite-looking animals in the world. Their feathers have been used in tribal head-dresses, not only as a sign of power but also to give a striking appearance to the wearer, making him stand out and indicating strength, wisdom and proficiency. But for a raptor, its plumage is its lifeline to successful hunting. The hawk will keep it in tip-top condition, thus allowing for optimum manoeuvrability when in flight. No matter how big and powerful a raptor may appear, without well-groomed feathers it will never perform to the best of its ability, so much of its waking time is spent therefore undertaking complete feather management.

In captivity, the falconer is also constantly concerned with the condition of his bird's plumage. Bent feathers should be instantly repaired using a brass straightener and those which have broken mended by imping, a skill which any austringer, as a keeper of broadwinged or shortwinged hawks is called, must master. A hawk held in captivity should be offered a bath regularly, as this will encourage grooming and help in keeping her feathers in perfect condition. The falconer should examine her daily, looking for the first signs of illness and of the dreaded bumblefoot, which one can do a great deal to prevent.

The Harris hawk is a diurnal bird of prey, which means it is active and hunts during the day. It is among the most sensational flyers and gracefully skilled predators. Harris hawks are solely carnivorous and have a powerful hooked upper mandible, which is just one of many striking features of this hawk as it is in all other raptors. This pointed hook (see

photo 2), is designed to pierce the flesh of captured quarry, which it does as easily as a hot knife through butter. Found on the base of the upper mandible is the cere (photo 2) upon which the nostrils or nares are situated. This soft flesh, which is often yellow, extends onto the face, and lines the mouth. The legs or tarsus (photo 3) are extremely powerful and covered with varying scaled patterns which act as protection. In some species, such as the true eagles, the flank feathers cover the whole leg, but those on the Harris hawk end high up, leaving much of the leg exposed. The birds have large, powerful feet, with four toes on each. The middle and back toes are the most powerful, designed for seizing and holding down captured prey.

Birds of prey come in a broad spectrum of sizes from the small falconets such as the African pygmy falcon (*Polihierax semitorquatus*) which weighs approximately 100 g (3½ oz) to the Andean condor (*Vulture gryphus*), the largest flying bird on earth with a wingspan of 3 m (10 ft). Raptors can be found on all continents except Antarctica, and in varied habitats, including deserts, forests and cities. They generally live at lower densities than other birds, and are extremely sensitive to human-induced changes in their environment. Any alteration in land use or other activity which reduces wildlife populations will inevitably affect birds of prey, which depend on other wildlife for survival. Persistent chemical pollutants which enter the

(2) The hooked upper mandible, the nares and the running of the cere

(3) The legs/scales, feet and flank feathers

bloodstream of potential quarry can ultimately cause devastating damage to the raptors themselves.

The Harris hawk was discovered by the great American naturalist and artist, John James Audubon, and named after his close friend Colonel Edward Harris, who was with him when he first saw it. Audubon was born in 1785 in Santo Domingo, now Haiti, and educated in Paris. He emigrated to the USA at eighteen. He spent his time travelling America collecting and painting the extensive wildlife around him. By 1825 he had compiled a beautiful set of bird paintings, but US publishers were not interested in their publication so he moved to Britain. He painted from real life and his compositions were startling in their minute detail. *The Birds of America* was published in Britain in eighty-seven parts during 1827–38. On his return to the USA in 1839, he published a bound edition of the plates with additions. He died in 1851.

Appearance

The Harris hawk is the only hawk in the genus *Parabuteo*. The name literally means 'similar to buteo' – large birds with thick bodies, broad wings, and somewhat rounded tails. The Harris hawk is long-legged and long-tailed. It is predominately dark brown, often appearing black when seen at a distance. It reveals large chestnut patches on the shoulders and

legs when perched, and in flight the wings also have a chestnut coloration. Immature birds have light eyes, which turn to dark brown when they get older.

Photo 4 shows the juvenile bird, with its chocolate brown head and neck and sparse pale streaking. The belly is streaked white with pale chestnut barrings, with an overall coloration of chocolate brown. The leg feathers are a pale brown with chestnut barring. Upper-wing and under-wing coverts are chestnut, with dark centres to many of the feathers. The tail is of a dark brown with a narrow white terminal band. The adult bird

(5) Plumage of the adult Harris

(photo 5) has a chocolate brown head, chest and neck with sparse pale streaking. Under-wing coverts and leg feathers are of a chestnut colour. There are dark flight feathers above and below, with white undertail coverts. The tail is dark brown, with a white terminal band.

Harris hawks are quite large birds. Their body lengths range from 45 to 65 cm (18–25 in) with wingspans of approximately 100–120cm (40–47 in). The females are a third larger than the males, and are therefore more powerful.

There are three subspecies: *Parabuteo unicinctus harrisi*, whose chest coloration is made up of predominantly dark feathers, *Parabuteo unicinctus unicinctus*, which is the smallest of the three, and *Parabuteo unicinctus superior*, the largest of the subspecies.

Eyesight

Like other diurnal birds of prey Harris hawks have forward-facing eyes and excellent vision. In comparison with the size of the skull, the majority of birds' eyes are large, but in raptors this is taken to extremes – some of the larger birds of prey have eyes which are as big as those of human beings.

Eyes of this size have a large area for capturing light via the cornea, which is further enhanced by its abrupt arching, setting the lens as far away as possible from the sensitive retinal area and giving an extended focal length with minimal telescopic vision. In comparison with other vertebrates, the retinal surface is more tightly packed with cells, especially with colour-sensitive cones in the two retinal fovea. This results in maximum clarity of the image bounced upon the retinal surface by the lens. It is believed that a raptor could read the headlines of a newspaper the full length of a football field away.

Their eyesight is not as well enhanced come nightfall, as they have a low density of light-sensitive rods in the retina. Their night vision is about the same as that of a human.

Their forward-facing eyes give raptors approximately 50° binocular vision and allows for greater accuracy and better judgement of distance both when stationary and in flight. Muscles operate the pupil apertures, which allows for fine, quick eye movements. This lends itself to accurate focusing and fast tracking. They can see in both black and white and colour and have a bigger spectrum of colours than humans.

They possess a transparent membrane, or third eyelid as it is often called. This fine membrane is drawn over the eye when the bird is flying at speed. For falcons such as the peregrine, which stoops at speeds well in excess of 100 mph, this membrane is essential, as if a fly hit the eye it would certainly blind the bird. It also serves to clean and moisten the cornea and to add nutrients.

A raptor relies on this excellent eyesight to locate, hunt and capture quarry with precise accuracy.

Hearing
Research into a raptor's sense of hearing has not been widely documented but diurnal birds of prey are sensitive to sound and it is thought that they have better hearing than humans. They hear a wider range of sounds and have the ability to detect their direction. Good hearing helps to locate quarry, predators, neighbours and partners. Owls have the best hearing: the barn owl, for instance, can successfully hunt purely by the ability to detect the quietest of noise, something a diurnal bird of prey could not do.

Smell
All birds of prey have a sense of smell, albeit a restricted one. A vulture's, however, is excellent, enabling it to pinpoint carcasses over many miles. Very limited information is available on diurnal raptors' sense of smell, but it is true to say that they rely more on their ability to see their prey than they do on their sense of smell.

Breeding
Harris hawks are not migratory birds; they nest year after year in the same vicinity. Nests are built mainly in saguaro cacti, arid mesquite and paloverde woodland. They are built approximately 3–9 m (10–30 ft) from

the ground and made from a simple platform of sticks, twigs, weeds and roots which are lined with moss or the like.

They are not generally monogamous. During courtship flights, the male goes into a vertical dive from approximately 200 m (650 ft) ending with an upward swoop to the back of the female, who will normally be perched within a tree. Copulation is then immediate. Occasionally two males will do this courtship display at the same time. Providing all three birds accept each other, the trio will remain together throughout the nesting season, which tends to ensure nesting success; should one male die, then the other is still available to bring food to the nest and help to protect it. This polyandrous behaviour is more apparent in Arizona, where there is a far greater male-to-female ratio. Breeding patterns are however extremely variable over the range of these hawks.

Nesting occurs from February through to October, and multiple broods are common in a single year. In Arizona, the eggs are laid from early March to mid-April with one to five eggs per clutch; three per clutch is normal. The eggs are usually either pure white or bluish white, but some may be speckled brown or lavender. Incubation is approximately thirty-five days. Feather growth is rapid, and by seventeen days the youngsters are sufficiently covered to begin wing exercising. The young birds will leave the nest and take their initial flight around forty days after hatching.

There is a distinctive pecking order amongst the juvenile birds in the wild. Although scrapping over food may be looked upon as playful fun, it is probably the first sign of dominance. Although the young, when able to do so, will go out within the pack in search of quarry, the older birds will often show their strength by nudging a youngster from its set-up point. An adult bird will, however, rarely attempt to steal a kill from a younger, less skilful bird.

It is reported that Harris hawks can live to approximately twenty years in the wild. Mortality is very low, due to their pack-hunting way of life. Solitary hunting hawks generally have a harder time capturing prey, as there are no companions to rely on should the quarry elude them, but the Harris's ability to flush and attack quarry in various ways gives it a far greater chance of success.

In its wild state the Harris hawk is an all-round skilled predator. It is an intelligent bird which is concerned with the success and livelihood of the pack. The manner in which they live and hunt in the wild can bring exciting scope to the modern falconer.

CHAPTER TWO

BUYING AND KEEPING A BIRD

Locating a breeder and purchasing a bird

Many seasons had come and gone since I last took up a female Harris hawk for the purposes of hunting. However, looking back over old journals and notes, it was clear to see the potential of the species, providing I was determined to work hard and nurture the bird's hidden talents.

For the season ahead I was looking forward to an alternative style of hunting, as I had recently been granted permission to fly within some woodland which was under pressure from grey squirrels, and other land which had the odd hare or two. I also had existing land which was consistently producing rabbits. The previous season had seen me partnering a male goshawk that, although a solid and consistent hunting bird, I did not feel would prove suitable for the season advancing. I felt that a female Harris hawk would offer greater versatility for what I was seeking to achieve and the quarry which would be available.

With successful captive breeding programmes throughout the UK, the modern falconer is now in a position to purchase a particular species to deal with particular quarry in particular countryside. For example, for rabbit and moorhen hawking one may choose a male Harris hawk with a hunting weight of approximately 1 pound 5–7 ounces as he would prove to be fast and nimble on the turn, with the capability to deal with such quarry. For rabbits in woodland, a male redtail might be better, as he may have the greater aptitude in this terrain. For hare, one would choose a female Harris hawk, as the added power and strength would help her bind onto this larger prey, and for duck and pheasant hawking a goshawk. Realistically, however, one would probably choose a bird which is versatile and able to fly a vast array of quarry.

Before obtaining any bird of prey, it is important to weigh up the land which you have available, the quarry on the land, and most importantly the amount of time you have available for your bird. These are serious considerations which must be taken into account when choosing a partner, as incorrect bird selection may well shorten your season. Falconers with limited mid-week flying could never justify the ownership of a goshawk or falcon, for instance, even if accessible land and quarry supported such species. Weather permitting, birds of this kind require flying every day.

The Harris hawk, although less demanding on the falconer, will, like all raptors, benefit from regular exercise, as the more she is flown the more self-belief she will have. This will be apparent when she takes on harder slips, showing the level of enthusiasm which is expected. An unfit, irregularly flown hawk will struggle in the field and miss or even decline kills which would have been well within her capabilities if she had been in adequate condition. A Harris hawk which is consistently being out-manoeuvred by quarry will become frustrated, as will the austringer. But one must never take out one's frustrations on the bird after a weak performance, as it is the austringer who is responsible for getting his bird trained, fit and ready for the field.

Once I had decided upon a female Harris hawk, it was time to think of general size, flying weights and potential breeders. I concluded that my bird should fly around the 1 kg (2 lb) mark as this, I envisaged, would bring both power and speed. Although this meant a smaller-looking bird, which for me was acceptable, it was vitally important that she had large powerful feet, especially as she was to hunt squirrels.

The next stage was to begin telephoning breeders I knew had an interest in Harris hawks. I drew up a list and started working my way through it. When I had reached the bottom it was apparent that only birds of the *superior* subspecies were being produced, which was little use to me as they would fly at a weight higher than I envisaged. This posed a slight problem, as to acquire the right bird I had to look further afield and enquire with breeders that I was not familiar with. I may be set in my ways, but, probably like most practising falconers, I prefer to do business with people I have a personal understanding with. I proceeded to ring breeders which were advertising in specialist publications such as the *Falconer's Magazine* and *Cage and Aviary Birds*. Again, it seemed that either these breeders were only producing young of the *superior* subspecies or I was not entirely satisfied with the answers I received to my questions. Although I am based in Essex, I would think nothing of driving to Scotland if I was assured of getting the right bird. However, this is a little too far to go on the off chance. Asking a breeder the right questions may save a great deal of time and unnecessary expense.

My hopes of purchasing a 1 kg (2 lb) bird seemed to be vanishing when I went off to see Paul Harris, a friend, falconer and breeder of many years. I had not spoken to him much over recent times but was aware that he bred kestrels and various other falcons; what I did not know was that he also bred Harris hawks. Some weeks previously I had ordered a kestrel from him, which was to be trained as part of my display team, and I was going to collect it. After completing the formalities, Paul asked if I would like to see his young Harris hawks, which were still in their breeding chamber. Peeking through the spy hole, I saw young Harrises which were ten weeks old. It was clear that these were not of the *superior* variety so I asked what weight the females would fly at. Paul's answer was around two pounds. I asked if any were still available, to which he replied yes. Without further delay, Paul was holding my deposit and my search was finally over.

One of the most important factors in successful and worthwhile hawk ownership is purchasing not only the right species and gender for the quarry and land available, but a bird which is healthy and strong and has been correctly reared. Most experienced falconers will be aware of breeders who have a reputation for producing excellent young. We will know them as honest, and more interested in supplying healthy birds than purely making money. But beginners may not be in this position and it is here that one could encounter problems. Those with limited experience will benefit from taking a competent falconer along to give an eyass a thorough going over. If one does not know another falconer then the following guidance may help when choosing a breeder.

Initially, you should gather a list of breeders who are within driving distance. This allows you to examine their whole set-up, aviaries etc. before a deposit is handed over. Work your way through the list, tele-phoning the breeders and asking questions which you feel are relevant to you. For instance, how big are the breeding quarters? As a potential buyer, I am looking for a nice-sized area so that the youngsters can get a little exercise. Those which have been reared in claustrophobic conditions with little or no room for movement are, in my opinion, not acceptable. I also prefer a breeding chamber to be fully enclosed so that the youngsters are unable to familiarise themselves with humans, and it should be posi-tioned away from the house so that they cannot associate with human voices. The spy hole which allows the breeder to log the youngsters' progress should be minuscule, and there should be a food shute in place so that they are unaware that it is a human who is the bearer of good tidings.

It is vital that one has total trust in the breeder. If a parent-reared bird is what you have ordered then you must be confident that that is what you will get. It is not at all difficult for any breeder to crèche-rear a bird and sell it as parent-reared. It is just as vital that the breeder rears the young on a good diet, i.e. quail and rodents, as this will give a young bird the nutritional values needed to help develop bones etc. Those which are reared on chick alone will not develop adequately.

You could also ask if references are available from previous purchasers. If I were a breeder I would be very interested in those who wished to pur-chase a youngster from me. I would vet them as much as they did me. I would be interested to hear from previous purchasers how the training was going and what quarry the bird was taking etc. Should the customer be happy, then I would ask if I could use them as a reference for future buyers. Not all breeders do this, but there are some who do.

Even for the more experienced austringer, purchasing a young bird is fraught with potential problems. Never try to save money when buying a bird of prey. Look for selling points and speak to as many breeders as you feel is necessary. Your final choice is likely to be correct if you follow the right procedures even if this does mean paying a little more. Never order a bird on the basis of words alone, never meet in a motorway service station to conclude a deal and never go ahead with a purchase that is to be delivered to you by courier. Make it perfectly clear to a breeder what it is you want, but above all, speak with authority.

Once you have found a breeder you feel happy with, ask if there are any guarantees about the bird's health. Breeders who value their reputation should guarantee the bird's health at the time of selling by offering an exchange or money-back policy and honouring their word should there be any reasonable dispute. Purchasing a hawk is a serious business. Buy the wrong bird and you will have an expensive problem. If it is imprinted (not parent-reared and therefore used to humans) and screams for either attention or food, you will find it extremely difficult to sell on, whilst if it has certain medical problems then you will have expensive veterinary bills. The guarantees I have mentioned should also apply to older birds purchased from a magazine advertisement. It may be that the seller has just cause to want to part with the bird, but it is certainly wise to ask for certain guarantees.

The time came for me to pick up my bird from Paul. She was now twenty weeks old and ready to leave her parents. A quick phone call to Paul before I left home and I was on my way. Although I have had many birds throughout my falconry career, there is still a buzz of excitement whenever I purchase a new one. Many thoughts run through one's head. Will she be feather perfect? Will her feet be free from swelling and bumblefoot? Will she be a pleasure to handle or will she be temperamental? And the one thought which we all no doubt have: will she develop into more than just a capable bird – in other words, will she be something special? I think all falconers hope that a new bird will be the golden bird we all subconsciously dream of owning.

On arrival at Paul's I was asked if I would like to join him whilst he caught up my bird. I like to see a bird caught up quickly and with minimal fuss as this alleviates stress. Often, the parents will get a little aggressive when their territory is invaded so it is wise for the breeder to have a degree of protective clothing on. Into the chamber went Paul, protected with a thick jacket and armed with a large net. With little more than a blink of an eye my bird was caught and brought inside for me to check over. A breeder with nothing to hide should allow you to examine the bird. Never allow the hawk to be placed directly into a box; this would certainly arouse my suspicion.

There are certain basic guidelines which one must address which will help confirm that the bird about to be purchased is both healthy and strong. Although we are unable to tell what is going on inside a hawk, we can see the outside and it is here where you must be thorough in your examination. My inspection began by just observing her at a distance. I then moved in and began by looking at her eyes. They ought to be wide open, clear and bright, which they were. Next, the nares. One is looking to ensure that there is no discharge, as this may indicate a chill, whilst at the same time checking the upper and lower mandibles for cleanliness, cracks and alignment. Make sure there is no damage to the cere area, as this may obstruct breathing. Next determine whether there is any foul odour coming from the bird's mouth, as this could indicate a stomach problem. Open each wing to make sure there are no restrictions or abrasions to the undersides, then closely examine the legs, which should be clean and straight with no redness, abrasions or swelling. Next the feet. Again it is vital that there is no redness, swelling or scabbing. They should be perfectly clean to allow a thorough inspection. If they are not, clean them with warm water and cotton wool.

Once I was satisfied that the feet were clear and that her talons were not worn to the quick but nicely formed, I put on a gauntlet and offered my hand into each foot to check the strength of her grip. Next came an overall inspection of the plumage. I was looking for feather perfection, with no broken, bent or missing feathers. I also like to see the plumage shining and free from dirt or faeces. Finally I had a quick feel of the keel bone before I attached the anklets and jesses. It was clear that the bird was in good condition, so I was happy to conclude the deal and go ahead with the purchase.

It is at times like these that one is glad to know the reputation of a breeder. We can be assured that the new bird is healthy, as the breeder has shown due diligence throughout the rearing. It is pleasing to know that the hawk has been bred in suitable surroundings, is fully parent-reared, if this is what was asked for, and has been fed a top-quality diet. The end result is a superb-looking specimen. Paul had done a grand job and I was totally happy with my new bird, which I named Ami.

Although a beginner should be able to carry out these basic checks, if you are at all unsure, the best advice is to take somebody along with you who does have the ability to recognise any problems.

Luckily, most breeders in the UK are honest and strive to produce excellent young. There is far more competition nowadays than there was five or ten years ago. Young of the year which have been reared on a quality diet in suitable breeding chambers may cost a little more, but I for one would not hesitate to pay slightly over the odds knowing that I have the makings of a good bird.

You must remember that the newly purchased eyass will have only seen a human briefly whilst an identification ring was put onto her leg. From the moment she is caught up, her life will change drastically. My policy is to check the bird over and get her home as soon as possible so she can settle.

(a) Flag of Egypt

(b) Flag of Ecuador

(c) Arms of Libya

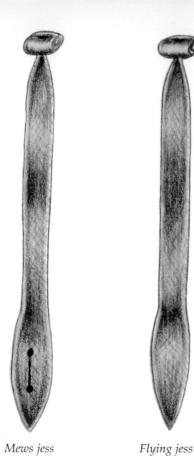

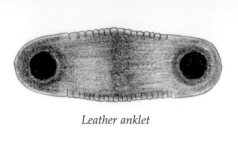

Leather anklet

*Anklet secured around leg
with brass eyelet*

Mews jess   *Flying jess*

(d) Aylmeri anklets and jesses

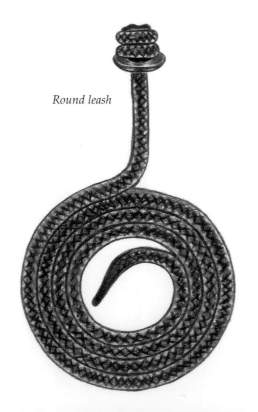

Round leash

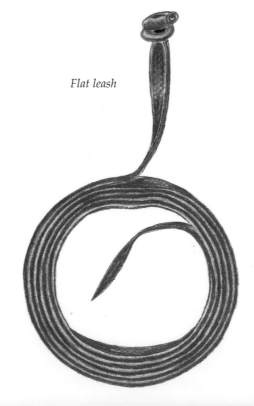

Flat leash

(e) Leashes

One has to think of how one is going to transport the young bird home from the breeder's. She will not be like a puppy or kitten, weak and capable of doing little more than sleep. She will be immensely strong, and given the chance will thrash about and do everything in her power to get out. The easiest and safest way is to go armed with a large, strong cardboard carton with a soft cushion or blanket lining its bottom. This will prove comfortable for the bird and help her keep a grip throughout the journey. Put some air holes along the bottom of the box; putting them higher up may cause the bird to bate, as she will be able to see daylight and detect movement. Make sure the box cannot tumble around your car should you need to brake hard or swerve. Transporting an older bird should be simplicity itself. If she is used to sitting on a perch, she can be placed in a wooden travelling box or else hooded on a portable bow perch or sturdy cadge.

Suitable weatherings, materials and design

Before a new arrival can be brought home from the breeder, there must be suitable living quarters firmly in place. To buy a raptor or an owl on impulse with little or no thought about its housing is just stupid. A bird of prey is entitled to appropriate living quarters just as much as a puppy. I am sure nobody would even think of purchasing tropical fish without first purchasing a satisfactory tank.

A hawk's living quarters should be as comfortable as possible, as the bird will be spending a great deal of her resting time inside. A weathering will benefit from a sloping felted roof. If the side panels are made from larch-lap, they should also be fully proofed with felt, as this will prevent draughts and give adequate strength against inquisitive foxes. Many people like to style the outside of the weathering so that it is presentable and complements the rest of the garden. If the panels are of a higher quality than larch-lap, a thick coat of wood preserver will not only finish it off nicely, it will give the timber added protection. Pretreated timber will benefit from being treated again, especially the up-stand posts which are sunk into the ground to hold both the side and back panels firmly in position. This can be done simply by sitting the wooden stands in the preserver for approximately twenty-four hours. The preserver is induced into the post, giving total wet-rot protection.

For as long as I can remember, there has been intense debate as to the design of suitable living accommodation for a bird of prey, and experienced falconers differ quite considerably in their opinions on design and measurement. There are, however, important elements which we must all bear in mind before construction can begin. For me one of the most important is size. Because I am quite tall I require a weathering to be approximately six feet in height. This allows for easy access at cleaning time and helps me avoid a pain in the lower back due to too much bending. Equally important is the position of the construction itself. To avoid the risk of feather plucking, usually a consequence of boredom, it is advisable to position your weathering in such a way that the bird has something of reasonable interest to look at during the day. The length of the garden ought to be fine.

The construction must be hardy, taking into account the heavy winds which it will face from time to time. It goes without saying that the roof should be water-tight, thus keeping the inside dry. Some hawks are prone to catching a disease known as aspergillosis (see page 100). A green residual membrane forms on damp, deteriorating timber, and this gives off and circulates deadly spores which the bird breathes in. These spores cause deterioration of the lungs. Birds diagnosed with this awful disease normally die. Fortunately, unlike redtails, goshawks and snowy owls, Harris hawks are not particularly prone to this fatal disease but they are, as I have already said, highly prone to frostbite. It is vital therefore that you keep the inside of the weathering from falling below freezing point. Placing a thermostatically controlled heater inside is ideal, especially if situated approximately 60–90 cm (2–3ft) above the bird's head. The front of the weathering will also benefit from some sort of covering, which can be as simple as a heavy-duty plastic blind which is pulled down to cover the whole of the open-fronted section during the coldest nights.

I do not like to admit it, but I take no pleasure in building aviaries. I am not orientated to building work and would undoubtedly struggle if

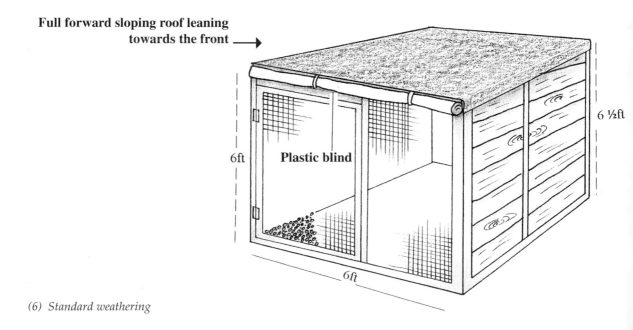

(6) Standard weathering

I did not have the help of friends who are. I do not have the skill to make sure that my new construction fits snugly together, is straight and looks presentable. Living on the Cambridgeshire Fenlands, the wind always seems to blow twice as hard as it did when I resided in Essex. Stronger constructions are therefore so much more important and must be left only for capable tradesmen. Unless you have a good understanding of basic building and design, get help from someone who does, as this will save both time and unnecessary expense.

For the arrival of Ami, a new weathering was needed, and after giving careful consideration as to its placement, all the materials were purchased from a large DIY warehouse. From past experience I knew it would take approximately two days to complete, so we set to work early one Saturday morning, two weeks before Ami was due. I feel it is important to give a weathering some time to settle down, just in case further work needs to be carried out.

The weathering which was to house my new hawk was built with three solid sides and a full, sloping roof which leans to the front (see fig. 6). A length of plastic guttering was fixed to the front to catch rain-water, which ran into a large container. A hardy door was made, to which a thick-gauge wire mesh was tacked. Before the inner floor could be lined, proofing work had to be carried out both internally and externally so as to protect my hawk thoroughly when tethered inside, as keeping poultry, my premises are frequently visited by foxes. Initially they are attracted to my chickens, but I am sure they would not hesitate to kill one of my birds given half the chance. Over the years I have heard many horror stories of birds being badly maimed and even killed by foxes whilst tethered to their perch inside their living quarters. We should all be aware of the devastation which foxes cause to livestock, and the falconer ought to feel a sense of duty to protect his bird in whatever way is necessary. The loss of a bird to a fox is, in my opinion, solely the fault of the falconer. There can never be any excuse for allowing something which is so easily avoided. Carrying out adequate proofing measures to stop these pests entering our weatherings is quite simple to do and far more cost-effective than purchasing a new bird and starting from scratch.

Once the main structure was complete, we excavated approximately 30 cm (1 ft) of earth internally and laid a heavy-duty wire mesh. The edges were bent upwards and tacked to the bottom of the larch-lap panels using staples. The mesh was then covered with the extracted soil and on top of the soil, we spread pea shingle. Around the exterior perimeter heavy paving slabs were placed on a bed of sand, as foxes are known to dig where the ground and panel meet so it is here that reinforcement is required. Proofing to such a degree may seem a little excessive, but most shrewd falconers will adopt these extensive measures and the beginner is well advised to do so as well. Do not learn the hard way.

The floor of the weathering must be lined with a suitable material. Once again, there is a difference of opinion among experienced falconers. There is a choice of turf, carpet, wood chips, silver or play-pit sand, astroturf and pea shingle. In making your decision, you must bear in mind that your weathering will need to be thoroughly hosed clean two or three times per week. So let us look at each lining individually.

- *Turf.* For many people, lining the bottom with turf is quite acceptable. It is easily washed clean and easily managed. However, during the winter months I have found that the grass becomes a little muddy, as a direct result of regular hosing and foot traffic, and a muddy weathering means a muddy bird. Her feet and primary and tail feathers will be constantly dirty, making extra work for the keeper. For this reason alone I find turf an unacceptable material. It will not withstand the abuse it will undoubtedly receive.

- *Carpet.* The only time I will ever use carpet is if a new bird is brought home from the breeders and tethered, and thrashes about a little more than normal. This can damage the tail and primary feathers, and a soft bed of carpet inside will obviously cushion them and eliminate this risk. But as a long-term lining, I think not. It is time-consuming to keep carpet clean, if it is possible to keep it clean at all. The fibres will house bacteria and it will look filthy thirty minutes after it has been painstakingly scrubbed.

- *Wood chips.* Although wood chips look very neat and attractive lining the bottom of a weathering, I would not use them. Wood chips are a breeding ground for mites and parasites and can cause aspergillosis. For this reason alone, I am put off them.

- *Sand.* I have known a few falconers use sand, but my advice is not to do so. It can get in between the hawk's toes, causing discomfort, and beneath her scaly feet, possibly causing sores and abrasions. Should it get wet or damp, it will discolour the tail and primary feathers, which will be hard to keep clean. Sand can also render the jesses, swivel and leash uncomfortable to handle. Silver sand is expensive, and like play-pit sand it is not possible to hose it clean. I would also worry about gusts of wind blowing particles into the bird's eyes and nares. There is also the risk that it will stick to the hawk's food if she is fed inside the weathering, and congest her crop.

- *Astroturf.* Many a falconer has lined the bottom of his weathering with this material, but I do not think it is a good idea. Astroturf is very difficult to keep clean; a hawk which is fed in the weathering will leave pieces of meat in between the fibres, and once this meat hardens, it is extremely difficult to remove. During the summer months it will attract blue- and greenbottles, which will lay their eggs on the decaying dry food matter – something that must be avoided. Astroturf is also expensive to purchase and hard work to manage.

- *Pea shingle.* This is my favourite lining by far. It is inexpensive to purchase and easy to hose down and keep to the standard necessary. When it is initially laid, it will contain excess sand, which can be simply hosed away. Before routine cleaning give the shingle a spray of Virkon S, a disinfectant which poses no threat to a bird's health, before washing it thoroughly away.

If space permits, you could construct a moulting or free-flight mews, which is far larger than the average weathering and has many more benefits. If perches are set at different heights the hawk gets a little exercise, which is especially good during the long summer moulting months when she is not flown at all. It will also alleviate boredom, as she will not be confined to one point. It is important for the Harris hawk keeper that his bird is able to get high off the ground so as to avoid frostbite during the cold winter months. But you should never allow your hawk freedom of flight until she is fully trained and manageable. Once trained, you can simply walk into the enclosure and call her onto the fist without fear of her thrashing about and risking feather damage. An ideal moulting pen would be similar to the floor plan shown in fig. 7.

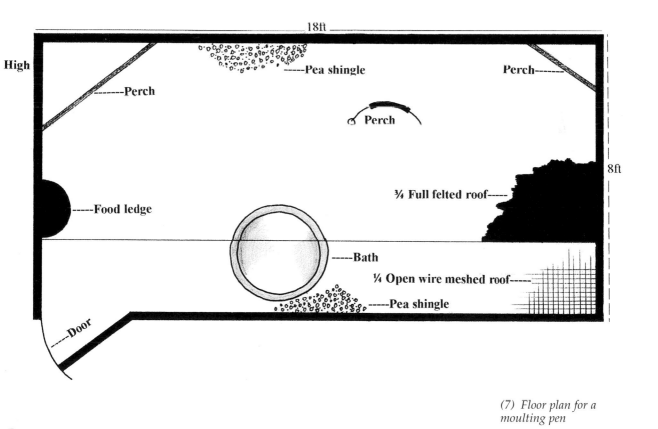

(7) Floor plan for a moulting pen

For many people, however, an outbuilding of this size would not be practical, so if you want to moult out your hawk in free flight or allow her to be untethered throughout the year, you have no option but to modify your weathering. This can be simply done by using a little imagination. First, a standard weathering is on the small side so it is important not to overcrowd such a confined area. I find that the average Harris hawk tends to remain reasonably calm throughout the moult, so one does not have to worry too much about fixed baths and food shutes. Personally, I would attach some fine bounce netting internally over the wire mesh just in case the bird shows signs of being temperamental whilst her weight is up. This will stop damage to the feet, cere and plumage. Fix a few perches inside at different heights to give her platforms to hop onto. Exercise will be somewhat limited, but a little may be better than nothing.

Whatever the weathering is made of it will not last for ever. It will need to be examined for defects and maintained on a regular basis. A routine overhaul will keep it in fine condition and ensure that it gives many years of use.

Falconry equipment

Just as important as having a new bird's living quarters firmly in place prior to it being brought home from the breeder, is having a full range of suitable equipment and accessories. The practising falconer may already have some of the equipment necessary to train and maintain a new hawk, but the beginner must work out exactly what is required and purchase a complete range accordingly.

Most experienced falconers will be familiar with the majority of equipment suppliers and have their current catalogues. They are then able to determined which supplier offers greater value for money. Unless the novice knows another falconer or is a member of a falconry club, however, he will not be in this position and choosing the right supplier from so many will be little more than a question of trial and error. It is important to find a supplier who is approachable and who treats each purchaser as an individual, with individual needs. Companies such as my own Eagle-Owl Falconry in Cambridgeshire and Crown Falconry, based in Derbyshire, are two such suppliers. Here you will not only receive professional advice, but you will also be assured of an excellent after-sales service.

Falconry equipment which is made to a high standard is not going to be cheap, ask any experienced participant. As always my advice is to purchase the best that your budget will allow and look after it, and it will serve you well season after season.

Below is a checklist of the equipment required to house, train and maintain a hawk successfully.

- anklets and jesses
- swivel
- leash
- perch
- gauntlet
- bells
- hood, if applicable
- creance
- lures
- bath
- scales
- telemetry receiver and tag

You will also need various sundries, such as a feather straightener, Virkon S, a needle, files and clippers.

Anklets and jesses *(See colour plate d)*
I am always amazed at the vast numbers of anklets and jesses which we sell in our shop and via mail order to falconers of all levels. Making these simple items of equipment would have been taught to you if you had attended a course and you should now be in a position to tailor-make these items for your bird to an acceptable standard.

Falconers tend to use kangaroo leather, which is immensely strong yet adequately supple. Its suitability, however, is reflected in its price. Brass eyelets are also required to hold the anklet firmly around the bird's leg.

To make anklets and jesses you will require in addition to the leather, brass eyelets, a leather punch and a closing tool. All accessories can be purchased from your supplier and should be in your falconry kit.

Swivels
Swivels are available in many weird and wonderful designs, and are made from various metals. Many, I find, are not practical for falconry purposes and are best avoided. It is vital to use a top-quality swivel which is constructed in either brass or stainless steel. Most experienced falconers, myself included, prefer stainless steel. Make sure you purchase the correct size swivel for the bird it is intended for. This can be ascertained by a quick telephone call to your supplier.

Leashes *(See colour plate e)*
This is another item of equipment which even the beginner should be able to make. Once again, there are various materials available which could be used, but braided terylene is in my opinion the best as it remains supple for longer periods. Leashes which are made from leather are now outdated and dangerous to use. Brittle leather can easily snap under bating pressure, and your bird could become snagged in a tree and die. Most

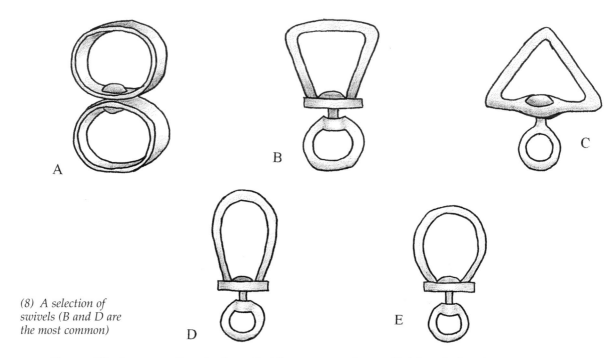

(8) A selection of
swivels (B and D are
the most common)

suppliers will give you the choice of either a round or a flat leash; beginners will probably find the round design far easier when it comes to tying
a falconer's knot.

If you have been shown how to make your own leash, you can buy a 25
or 50 m roll of terylene from a falconry supplier or a ship-chandler. In the
long run this will save many pounds, and you will have new leashes as
and when required.

Perches (*See colour plate f*)
Over the years falconers tend to accumulate an array of both block and
bow perches. For a Harris hawk you will need a bow perch of the correct
size for the bird. It is important that her tail feathers do not trail the
ground when she is sitting on the gripping section.

Bow perches are intended to simulate the natural surfaces which the
bird would be used to in the wild. Broadwings and shortwings would
benefit from a design that simulates the curvature of a tree branch. Falcons
and owls, on the other hand, would be better suited to block perches, as
they are accustomed to flat perching platforms in the wild.

Bow perches are made in many designs using various materials. The
D-shaped bow illustrated in fig. f (colour plate section), should be
constructed from stainless steel and preferably have a rubber or leather
gripping point with a stainless steel tig-welded tethering ring. Such a
perch will be attractive and robust, giving one years of use.

The gripping surface is an important feature of perch construction.

Until recent times the falconer had only the choice of leather, astroturf and cord binding. Leather, if it is not regularly greased with a suitable dressing, will go brittle, especially if it is regularly left outdoors to face the elements. Although astroturf is a proven bumblefoot preventer, it is laborious to keep clean, especially if the hawk is allowed to eat her food on it. Cord was one of my favourite surfaces but again it was very difficult to keep clean. Many falconers do not like cord because the bird is able to catch a talon between its windings, causing severe injury and excruciating pain. Recently, Crown Falconry has developed a perching surface that is moulded from rubber, which the proprietor kindly offered me the opportunity to assess. I found the rubber exceptionally easy to keep clean, and as water will not damage it, it will give years of use. Moreover, it was kind to the hawk's feet. This bow and those finished in leather are now the only perches which we use here at Eagle-Owl Falconry.

Most falconers have a perch in the weathering which is only moved for the purposes of cleaning, and a second for use on the weathering lawn. For the beginner trying to save money, this is not necessary and the perch used in the aviary can also be used on the lawn. It is worth mentioning that you should have a perch with heavy base plates, known as an indoor or portable perch. This comes into its own when a sick hawk needs to be brought indoors, maybe because it has a chill. A perch which is designed to be pushed into the ground would, in this instance, be of little use. Remember, you could save a sick bird's life by bringing her indoors overnight out of draughts and cold.

Falconry gauntlets (See colour plate g)

These items should only need to be bought a few times throughout your entire falconry career. I still use my first adult-sized gauntlet, which is approximately seventeen years old and still going strong. This is probably because it is made from quality buckskin leather and crafted to a professional finish. In addition to these two major facets, the time I have taken caring for it over the seasons has obviously been worthwhile.

Although falconry gloves come in various lengths and thicknesses, it is not necessary to buy a new glove for every new bird. The beginner would therefore benefit from purchasing a full-length, double-thickness gauntlet, as this will serve all birds other than eagles.

Falconry bags (See colour plate h)

As with the falconry gauntlet, you do not need to purchase a new bag for every new bird. If you buy a top-quality bag in the first instance, and go on to maintain it adequately, then it will last for many seasons. Whatever bag you purchase, it is advisable to make sure it has a large game pocket and a detachable meat pouch for ease of cleaning. You will also require a strap, which will be classed as a separate item and will need ordering accordingly.

Bells

It is essential that your bird is equipped with sweet-sounding, purpose-designed falconry bells. They can be put around the hawk's legs with a leather bewitt, which is basically a bracelet, or onto one or both centre deck feathers which is often done using a medium thick guitar plectrum. I tend to use a tail mount to which a single bell is attached, as this leaves the legs freer. Harris hawks, like other hawks, tend to move their tails quite often. If the bird is in a tree the falconer will know instantly if she moves, as the bells will sound. This item of equipment is something that the practising falconer will probably have stored away, but the beginner may have to try various makes before he is happy with the tone produced.

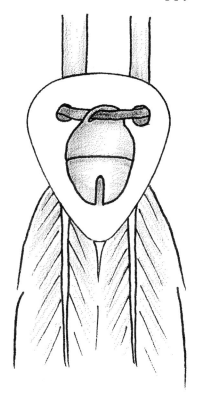

(9) Falconry bell on a tail mount

Hoods *(See colour plate i)*

Many falconers like to hood their Harris hawk, but I do not. In fact, I have never hooded a Harris in my entire falconry career. Hooding is useful when transporting a bird on a bow perch in the rear of a vehicle, as the hood puts her in complete darkness which keeps her at ease, thus eliminating the risk of bating. My own hawks are travelled to and from a venue in a sturdy wooden travelling box, which achieves the same result as the hood but suits me better.

If you prefer to hood your bird, then make absolutely sure that the hood is professionally made and fits the bird perfectly. If it is too big she will see daylight, which will achieve nothing, whilst if it is too tight it will inflict unnecessary pain when the braces are drawn, i.e. the hood closed around the bird's head, which may render the bird hood-shy. The plain Anglo-Indian hood illustrated in fig. i (colour plate section) is ideal for a Harris hawk.

Creances *(See colour plate j)*

The creance is basically a length of training line which is used once the hawk has been manned. It consists of a lathe-turned handle onto which 25 or 50 m of cord is wound. It is an essential piece of equipment, as it is the item that gets a young bird flying to the fist from a distance. Once again, the creance can last for years if it is adequately maintained.

Lures *(See colour plates k and l)*

In the UK it is illegal to use live quarry to encourage a young bird to kill. The falconer therefore has no other option but to use make-believe quarry, known as lures. There are two types, the swing lure and the rabbit lure. Both can be shown to a Harris hawk, but the way in which they are introduced is important.

The rabbit lure is obviously intended to simulate a rabbit. It is made from artificial fur, which is packed with toy filling. It will have both a head end and a tail end, which should be easily distinguishable. The food is tied towards the head end so that the hawk gets used to striking the vital part of live quarry.

The swing lure is intended to simulate flying quarry. The actual pad is much smaller and lighter than the rabbit lure and is made from strong leather, which again is packed with toy filling. There will be a place on the pad's body where you can attach a variety of cured wings. These are sold separately and familiarise the bird with different quarry colorations.

As I have said, it is vital that one introduces the lures individually and at the correct time so as not to confuse the hawk. I wait until the bird is flying the full length of the creance before I show her the rabbit lure. Once she is leaving the perch and hitting the rabbit without hesitation, I will move on to the swing lure. The bird is normally flying free at this stage. Beginners will be shown the precise methods to adopt on any good falconry course.

The lure will come into its own if a bird is stubbornly sitting in a tree and refusing to fly back to the fist. In this case the sudden showing of either lure is often all that is required to bring the bird back under control.

Birds have been known to bruise their feet by striking pads which are too heavy. It is therefore vital that the lure pad is not filled with sand or the like, as this heavy filling is asking for trouble. Either lure may sometimes contain a sealed bag filled with sand particles, for optimum weight and balance. This is perfectly acceptable just so long as the whole thing is not filled in this way.

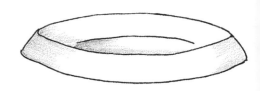

(10) Hawk baths

Baths

It is important that your bird takes a bath on a regular basis. Bathing encourages preening and natural feather management. An adequate bath can be purchased from your equipment supplier, who will tell you the size required for the bird. For a Harris hawk an ideal bath should measure approximately 90 cm (3 ft) in circumference, with a middle depth of approximately 13 cm (5 in). Hawk baths are generally moulded from glass fibre and available in various designs, although round more often than not will be the normal shape stocked by suppliers. Only a bath designed with birds of prey in mind should be used; do not be fooled into using upside-down plastic or rubber dustbin lids etc.

Scales

The fine balancing act of feeding a hawk the correct volume of food to attain and maintain a stable flying weight is the most important aspect of hawk ownership. Correct weight control can make the difference between

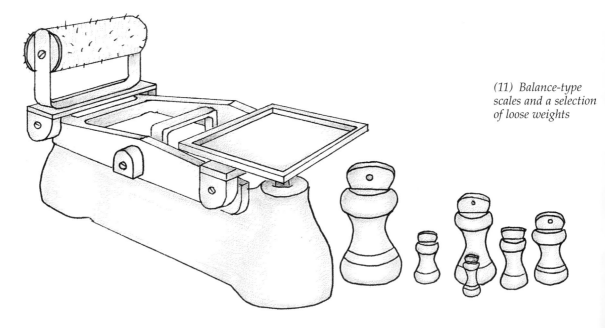

(11) Balance-type scales and a selection of loose weights

life and death. It will therefore come as no surprise that the scales you use must be top quality and totally reliable.

Many falconers now use custom-designed digital scales or the balance type with a selection of loose weights. Balance scales like those used by grocers will need converting so that the hawk has something to sit on whilst a reading is being taken. Never use the old-fashioned spring variety as they are too unreliable.

Although there are other factors which determine a hawk's performance, such as weather conditions, fitness, amount of exercise and the time of day when she is flown, weight is vital, and quality scales are an essential aid.

Telemetry systems

I would not consider flying a hawk without using a telemetry system. The modern falconer has many systems to choose from, some good and some not so good. Most of the modern systems which I have been able to field test have proved to be more or less satisfactory, but in recent times we at Eagle-Owl Falconry have favoured the Biotrak system which we find easy to use, compact and reliable. A telemetry system is not going to be cheap,

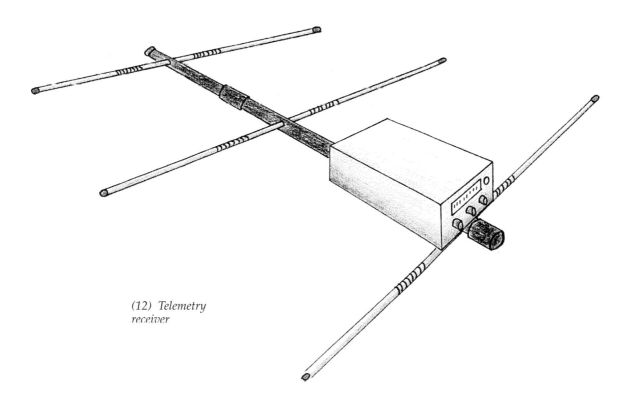

(12) Telemetry
receiver

(12a) Telemetry transmitter

as in addition to the receiver you will also require a transmitter. The transmitter, or tag as it is often called, is what the hawk carries, either around the leg or attached to the tail by a tail mount. Before you purchase a system, try to field test all those which are in your price range until you are happy with your final choice. The annual British Falconry Fair is the best place to carry out field testing due to the many systems on display.

Many falconers do not use telemetry, especially those who fly Harris hawks, as they believe that the odds of losing such a species is minimal. I have to disagree, and the wise falconer will never fly without it.

Diet and food care

We should all be aware that trying to manage a bird on an inadequate diet could have severe consequences. Imagine a healthy strong human being fed solely on junk food for a prolonged period. His health would most certainly deteriorate, his bones would become weak, his strength would dwindle, he would appear gaunt and pale, and he would suffer from tremendous abdominal pain before possibly eventually dying. No doubt we have all had periods when we have lived off such food, for a time, but we can give our bodies nutrients when necessary. A hawk held in captivity cannot do so and is dependent on you. If you want your bird to perform well, feed her well. If you want her looking her best, feed her the best. These are basic lessons which all beginners should learn. One must take feeding time seriously, as correct feeding will keep her internally healthy, which will be reflected externally in fine-looking plumage, bright sparkling eyes and the will, grit and determination to chase and kill quarry.

A very good selling point for any breeder is the fact that his youngsters have been reared on a top-quality diet. As a purchaser, this is something which I always look for. I feel it is vitally important that the mother of any youngster I may eventually purchase has been fed a balanced diet to keep her healthy and strong, and that the same diet is made available to her growing young.

All birds of prey are born with delicate bones, but the Harris hawk's are more delicate than most. Many may break a leg even before they have been manned due to excessive bating, whilst many more will go on to sustain such injuries during their first competitive season. Those young-sters which have been reared on a healthy, balanced diet will be in a far safer position, as their bones will be naturally hardier. It is then the duty of the falconer to see that his bird continues to receive a correct diet which is cleanly presented, both during the flying season and afterwards, when the hawk is put down for the moult.

One major issue which faces many beginners is where to purchase food. The majority of bird farms, and a few pet shops, will offer a limited supply of day-old chicks, rats and mice. The quality at such outlets is sometimes low, whilst the price is often quite high. Although it does not suit every-body, I have to say that delivery via courier is nowadays extremely reliable, and this is the way we now purchase our food here at Eagle-Owl Falconry. Our suppliers offer us a broad spectrum of foods at an excep-tional rate, which I believe is much the same for those who purchase in smaller quantities. The only disadvantage in using a courier is that no delivery time is given. Should this prove to be inconvenient, and to most it will, then one has little alternative but to find a specialist supplier who is based within driving distance. This can often prove difficult, but providing one does not live in one of the remotest parts of the UK there will generally be one. And as long as our sport grows so will the number of outlets supplying food. It has also been known for falconers to invest in second-hand freezers, purchase food in bulk and sell it on to make a profit. This way one always has good stock and can make some additional money. If there is not an outlet close to where you live, then this may be worth thinking about.

Whatever your purchase arrangements, it goes without saying that the supplier should always maintain a constant supply of different foods. A half empty or empty freezer gives you limited or no choice and could put you in a predicament. It is not wise to use unreliable outlets, but then it is also not wise to run your stocks down too low. And always have a back-up outlet even if this means driving further afield than you would like.

The austringer should understand the values of the food he feeds his charge, as different foods will have different nutritional values, which could affect the bird's hunting weight tremendously. During the flying season, you will want your bird at a tight hunting weight to optimise her awareness and responsiveness to quarry and to the fist. You will also require your bird to fly strongly, without worrying about her falling ill due to undernourishment. Without adequate fuel inside her she will struggle to perform to the best of her ability and be hard pushed to work all day on a large field meet. Here are the foods normally fed to birds of prey by modern falconers.

Day-old chicks

Culled at a day old, chicks are the most common food given to birds of prey, and some birds are fed nothing else. I cannot understand this as they

(13) Day-old chicks

contain very little goodness. Rarely do we at Eagle-Owl Falconry use chicks, even though they do have the benefit of keeping a hawk at a tight flying weight. Personally, I prefer to use rabbit enhanced with a little nutritional supplement such as SA 37 to stabilise my birds at flying weight. Once a week, however, our hunting hawks will be fully cropped with foods that contain higher natural nutritional values, such as rats, mice or quails. This weekly crop boosts them with the essential goodness, which will keep them flying strongly over a long, hard season.

Day-old chicks contain a yolk sac that should be removed before it is fed, as the yolk will eventually discolour the bird's feet and cere.

The roughage content in a day-old chick is minimal and you may find that additional roughage is needed if the hawk has trouble casting.

Occasionally chicks can be contaminated with salmonella, which can kill the largest and strongest of hawks. Purchase only from reputable outlets where the chicks have been frozen correctly.

Grown-on chicks
These are basically larger chicks. Although they have a higher protein and calcium content, they still should not be used for continuous feeding. The roughage value on a grown-on is far superior to a standard chick but one should occasionally supplement with SA 37.

Feeding just day-old and grown-on chicks runs the risk of a hawk discarding other sources of food, as chicks are extremely palatable. This may lead to the bird becoming food temperamental, and it is wise not to use this food source exclusively.

(14) Grown-on chick

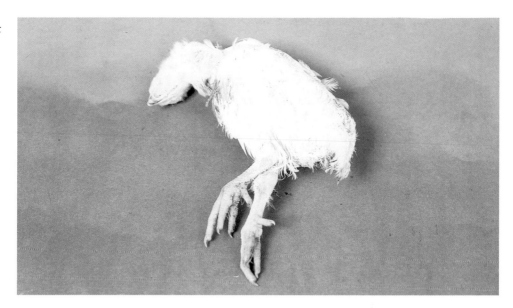

Rabbit

Rabbit is a food which is often gathered throughout the hawking season by the bird herself. As a result, the falconer may well have enough stocked away to feed her continuously throughout the moult. Rabbit does not have a high nutritional value, so it should not be fed exclusively, especially during the moult when new feathers are growing and quality food is more important than ever.

(15) Rabbit

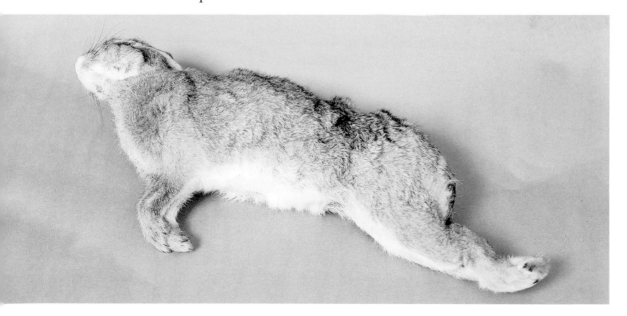

(16) Rats

Rat

Rat is an excellent food. It is easily acquired and simply prepared. It contains ample protein and other nutrients and is relatively inexpensive to purchase. More and more falconers tend to use weaner rats, which are much smaller and far less smelly when gutted. You will find it extremely difficult to hold a hawk at a tight flying weight during the hunting season because of the goodness found in this food, but give her the benefit of its superior quality once a week.

Mouse

Like rat, mouse is an excellent food source, and is readily available. The only disadvantage is the price. To feed such a food occasionally during the flying season and then continuously throughout the moult will not be cheap. Some austringers breed their own mice, which can be viable if it is done on a large scale.

(17) Mice

Quail

Like rat and mouse, quail is a top-quality food, but it is expensive to purchase. Quails do, however, contain many good nutrients which will complement your bird's diet. Again this is a food that many falconers tend to breed themselves.

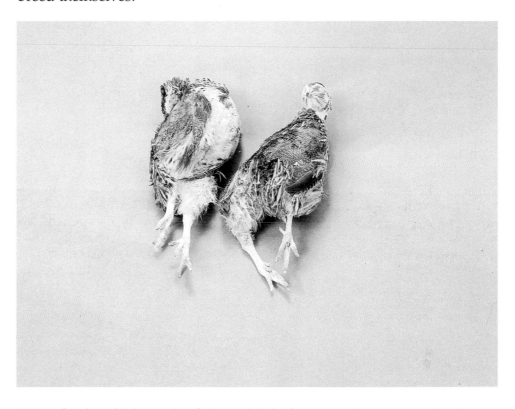

(18) Quails

Other foods which can be fed to a bird of prey are hare, game birds and squirrel. Squirrel is not easily come by and is tough, whilst game birds and hare generally end up on the falconer's table. Liver is ideal for a sick bird, as it contains iron and is easily digested whilst many use beef when coaxing an eyass to feed via the fist. Never feed road casualties or food whose history is questionable, and certainly never feed game which has been shot with a 12-bore, as lead shot will poison and or damage the hawk's gut. Know the origin of the food you feed.

Although it is vital that the austringer feeds his bird a good diet, it is just as important that you present the food correctly. Cleanliness of the highest order is needed; knives, chopping boards and hands ought to be clean as should the detachable meat pouch in your falconry bag.

A bird of prey is only as good as the fuel inside her. A lack of fuel could mean poor performances in the field. It could also result in the bird becoming ill and possibly dying.

Maintaining a healthy bird

Although it is common for falconers to disagree with one another quite regularly, I am sure we all agree that owning a bird of prey is a very serious, ongoing commitment which will not suit everyone. When the weather is at its coldest, and the wind is biting from all angles, the hawk at the bottom of the garden will still require feeding. She will need checking over for defects in equipment and to ensure that there is no physical impairment. During winter this is, for some, an unpleasant thought. Very few people feel any incentive to clean a bird's weathering thoroughly before getting ready for work themselves on a dark, frosty morning, whilst the damp, dark early evenings are just as unappealing. It is at this time of year that one's dedication is pushed to the very limit. Those who take on a bird of prey have important duties to carry out 365 days of the year. Not everyone who purchases a hawk in the summer will be there to talk of the flying season come the following March.

(19) A Harris hawk taking a bath

Before you buy a hawk, therefore, you must be fully aware of the challenge you are taking on. All beginners should attend a good course, as it is here that this important information will be passed on. Those who purchase on impulse, without thinking things through, all too often leave their birds in filthy surroundings, untrained and unfit. True falconers have passion for their sport and total respect for the birds under their care, whatever the weather or time of day.

Allocating time for your bird each day is important, so that you can thoroughly check her over for signs of deterioration in equipment or the weathering and possible illness. All the physical checks which were made at the breeder's when you initially purchased your bird should now be carried out daily. Although this does not take too much time once you are in the swing of things, be thorough, as it could save your bird from unnecessary suffering or even death. Some beginners see a large Harris hawk as a robust predator which is unlikely ever to become ill or sustain injury. If only this were true. A hawk with the slightest of chills can quickly deteriorate if appropriate antibiotics are not administered.

I feel privileged to own birds of prey and Ami, my new Harris hawk, will, just like my other birds, receive my undivided attention for the necessary period of time every day. During the course of a flying season I will be aware that she is more likely to break a leg, sustain injuries to her wings, snap or bend a vital flight feather, receive foot injuries, split her beak etc. During this period, therefore, I will be extra cautious and continually check her over. Should injury occur during the course of a field meet, I will cease flying and head straight back to the vehicle to administer the appropriate treatment. Always carry a first-aid kit (see page 104) so that if the bird has an open wound, for example, measures can be taken to help stop bleeding and possible infection. One season my redtail acquired a nasty bite from a rat. In my first-aid kit were all the items I needed to clean the wound until veterinary treatment could be given. Those austringers who choose to wipe the blood clean with their fingers and continue to fly will give an abrasion such as this the opportunity to go infectious. A first-aid kit is vital; never be without it.

It is encouraging to learn that some vets run short courses in avian first aid for those who are registered with their practice. This is invaluable to any falconer and I strongly recommend that you make enquiries and attend such a course. It could save your bird's life.

Of vital importance to the austringer is the state of his bird's plumage. Here one is in a position to assist the bird and encourage her to manage her own feathers by offering her the opportunity to bathe. Most Harris hawks take to the bath quite freely and, I am sure, look forward to a regular cleansing. Providing it is not too cold, it is wise to offer the bath early in the day so that the hawk has plenty of time to dry off. Never allow her inside the weathering overnight with damp plumage as she may easily catch a chill. After bathing the hawk will preen and oil the feathers, using the oil gland which is found above the two centre deck feathers. This oil will give her plumage sheen and protection.

Imping, the repair of damaged feathers, is a skill which the austringer must master. There are various ways in which a bird could damage a feather and the austringer should be familiar with, and able to deal with, any situation. The immaculate condition of a raptor's feathers are vital to her if she is to fly with optimum control and manoeuvrability.

Other sensitive areas are the talons and beak, which will need close monitoring and repair, a practice known as coping. Overgrown talons will require trimming, as there will be a danger of the bird piercing her own feet, which could lead to infection. After trimming, they should be repointed, as this will help her to bind onto quarry.

Successful coping requires a good set of needle files of various thicknesses and shapes. These can be purchased either from your equipment supplier or from any good hardware shop. You will also need some clippers. The stainless steel plier type used by vets is probably the best and can be purchased at any good pet shop.

Should damage be noted to the beak, then appropriate repairs should be carried out immediately, no matter how slight the damage may appear. If the upper mandible is allowed to overgrow it is more likely to crack and continue cracking, often at a prolific rate. Cracked or split mandibles offer excellent harbourage for food to decay. Simple filing immediately can avoid serious filing eventually.

Both imping and coping require a high level of dexterity. The beginner must be given hands-on experience, as this is the only way to learn properly. A well-structured falconry course is again invaluable here.

Also of concern are external parasites. Your bird ought to be sprayed at least twice a year using a pyrethrin-based insecticide such as Johnson's Anti-mite. Falconers tend to do this just before and after the moult. It is important to spray the bird's plumage thoroughly but without any entering her eyes or nares. Do not try to do this on your own as you will never do it thoroughly. Engage the help of a friend and cast the bird.

We all have a duty to look after the birds in our care. Should there be any signs of ill health then they should be seen by a qualified avian vet. It is important that your vet has experience with birds of prey and that he or she is willing to see your bird at short notice, including evenings, weekends and bank holidays.

CHAPTER THREE

THE DIARY

The first two weeks

On arriving home from Paul's, my first priority was to remove Ami from the cardboard travelling box and get her settled on the weathering lawn. It is my strong belief that the following few weeks are vital for the relationship between falconer and bird. Although the sun was shining it was not hot; in fact, it was a glorious September's day. Everything was calm except for the intrusive noise of magpies.

My journey home had been more than satisfactory; Ami had not thrashed around and there was little traffic to contend with. Earlier that morning I had sectioned off a corner of my garden which I hoped Ami would find private. It was shaded by overgrown trees and out of the winds which this splendid day occasionally produced. From this position she would be unable to see my chickens, my ducks or my ferrets, which were tirelessly play-fighting in their run. In fact there was nothing which could upset her, and after the disruption she had already suffered, it was vital she was not worried any more than absolutely necessary.

I took the cardboard box into my workshop. Although Ami had already been fitted with anklets and jesses, I needed to attach the swivel and the leash. Gingerly I opened the lid of the box, not quite knowing what to expect. A new arrival could at this stage either fly directly at you or remain still enough to allow you to take hold of the jesses. Thankfully Ami remained still. With my gloved hand, I carefully took hold of the leather jesses and slowly lifted her from the box. Suspended in mid-air, I gave her back support with my right hand until she was positioned, back down, on a soft towel on my work-top surface. I was now able to attach the swivel and thread through the leash.

The majority of Harris hawks I have owned have had a terrible tendency to pick, pull and even eat the strands of fibre which make up the leash. I have concluded that if I use a flat leash as opposed to a round one they tend not to ruin as many and often do not attack it at all. With Ami still on her back, but now with the leash and swivel attached, I lifted her from the table-top, again supporting her back with the ungloved hand and proceeded to walk her towards the weathering lawn, where a large bow perch was in position.

I do not see the benefits of attempting to get the bird sitting on the fist at this stage as this will do little more than add unnecessarily to the stress which she has already incurred. How much better to tether her to the perch and allow her to settle down and find her feet. I knelt down besides the perch and lowered Ami's back gently onto the ground, tying the leash to the tethering ring. She remained still momentarily, as though her back were glued to the grass. With a blink of an eye however, she took to her feet and sat erect to the side of the perch. Although she was sitting on her backside with both her mouth and her wings open she was none the worse for wear. Once I had assessed the situation and was happy that all was safe, I decided to leave her alone and retire indoors for a cup of coffee. From my lounge I was able to sit quietly and observe her every move, focusing closely on her with binoculars.

When a young hawk is initially tethered to a perch there is always the risk that she will thrash about, risking damage to both the primary and tail feathers. For this reason alone, many austringers do not allow a new bird inside the weathering immediately. If bating occurs, it is far safer that it is done on the lawn, as the grass will, to a degree, shield the feathers. If Ami still proved unpredictable in the evening, then I would place an off-cut of carpet in her weathering, as the coarseness of the pea shingle lining the floor could seriously damage her plumage. This carpet would be removed once she chose to sit on her perch and showed no signs of thrashing around.

(20) Ami settling on the weathering lawn

After allowing her a couple of undisturbed hours to settle, I felt it was time to tempt her onto the scales. It is important to weigh a bird as soon as possible, preferably within hours of arriving home. I needed to establish her fat weight as this would give me an educated guess – and it *is* only an educated guess – of her eventual flying weight. A young bird freshly taken from the parents should be at fat aviary weight, as she will have been on full rations. This should have been confirmed by feeling the keel bone at the time of purchasing. You must do this before allowing the hawk into the travelling box as this will determine if she is indeed at full weight.

It is quite feasible to sit a hawk on the scales, even if she is not yet sitting on the fist, but extreme patience will be needed. I took Ami into my weighing room, again hanging upside down and again shielding her back with my ungloved hand. I knew my next task would not be easy, but from previous experience, I also knew it would not be impossible. The scales were suitably positioned and I lifted Ami up onto my fist. Her initial response was immediately to bate off. Again I brought her onto the fist, only this time I applied light pressure to her back, which helped me balance her on the glove. After a light twisting of the fist, she applied minimal gripping pressure, which aided her balance. I moved her towards the scales and attempted to sit her on the custom-made T-perch. She had other ideas, however. My first attempt failed, so I tried again – and again, and again, each time thinking of easier sports I could have pursued, like golf. After numerous attempts, I finally managed to position one foot on the perch, and after endless coaxing and persevering, the second. It is at times such as these that the handler risks being footed by a nervous hawk. An eyass of the year will not be used to you touching any part of her torso and may object even more to being touched around the feet area. Always be on the defensive, as a hawk's foot movement is extremely quick.

Eventually, Ami took a half-hearted stance on the perch, appearing to be balancing more than gripping. I did manage to take a reading, however, which I recorded at 1014 g (2 lb 3¾ oz). I had thought she would be a little heavier than that as she appeared physically bigger and her keel bone had felt fat when I checked it at Paul's. I double-checked my scales, which were unquestionably correct; it was therefore obvious that my visual assumption was astray by a couple of ounces or so. I took Ami back onto the weathering lawn, tethered her and once again allowed her time to settle down.

For the next week or two I did not intend to do any physical manning or training with her. There are those who try endlessly to get the hawk sitting upon the fist the very day it is brought home from the breeders. I do not. Although their perseverance may pay off, it is often only after multiple bating and when the bird is all but exhausted. Remember, an eyass of the year which has been freshly taken from her parents will have no reason to accept you. Only after she has relaxed somewhat and is confident that you mean her no harm, and when her weight is coming down and she is being bribed with the offering of food will her acceptance begin to show. Even if she does sit on the fist the first day, it is extremely unlikely that she will bend her head in anticipation of food, especially if she is fat – as she ought to be. So what will one have achieved? The bird may have sat on the fist, which is really no major feat, but one will have a hawk which is highly stressed and unnecessarily exhausted. Being only the first day, this is not an ideal way to win an animal's trust. I intended to do little more than spend indirect time with Ami whilst she was on the weathering lawn, letting her observe me whilst I went about my business, even letting her discover my dog, which would be set at a distance. But this was as far as it went, at least until the bird ceased to bate and spread her wings whenever she was aware of my presence. Only then would I begin the intense manning process.

All in all it had been a pleasing first day. Ami had not damaged any feathers and, although it had been a daunting challenge, I had managed to record her first weight. She still preferred to sit on the ground as opposed to the top of the perch which, although not surprising, was worrying me. However, there were still a few hours or so before she had to be put away, so I decided to keep my fingers crossed and hope she would eventually hop onto the perch of her own accord.

I began preparing food for my other birds. Although I did not expect Ami to eat any offering, I did leave her with a piece of rabbit overnight. An eyass of the year which is fresh from the aviary should have enough fat reserve to go many days without feeding, so if the food was still where I had left it in the morning I would not be too worried.

Once my birds, chickens, ducks, ferrets and dogs had all been fed, and after finishing my other tasks, Ami was still sitting on the ground, so I had no alternative but to cushion the pea shingle in the weathering with a section of off-cut carpet. I left her a piece of rabbit inside before I went over to get her. I approached her very slowly and quietly on all fours, hoping she would not bate. Never tower over a new bird, as this will make you appear far more intimidating. As I got closer, she was on her guard, mandibles apart, wings wide open, and once again she was sitting on her backside. I took hold of the jesses, untied the leash and walked her to the weathering, supporting her back as she was once again suspended in mid-air by the jesses. I took her into her new home for the first time, lowered her back onto the carpet and tethered her securely to the perch. She immediately found her feet and began bating, so I made a quick exit, locking the door behind me. Luckily she ceased bating almost immediately. In a single day much had changed in Ami's life but all in all she had done extremely well.

The following day was again bright and mild. My two main objectives for that day were to take another weight reading and to see Ami sitting on her perch. My approach to the weathering was slow and quiet, as I did not want to startle her. Instead of advancing side on, I walked to the front of the weathering, standing at a distance of approximately 10 m (33 ft). This allowed her to see me directly at range. I then walked slowly towards her. I was pleased to see that she was actually sitting on her perch, but I noticed that she had not touched her food. As I got closer her wings began to open; my objective was to open the door and walk inside without a bate – almost impossible, I know, but well worth the attempt. Once I was at the door the first bate come. I quickly entered, untied the leash and carried her out into the open. Without further delay I took her into the weighing room and recorded a second weight of 978 g (2 lb 2½ oz), again after numerous attempts. I then placed her on the weathering lawn to settle whilst I carried out some maintenance work on my other aviaries.

This work took far longer than normal, as I had one eye constantly on Ami. Each time I made a bang with the hammer for instance, I would look to see if there was a reaction, as she would eventually have to be fully at ease whenever she heard sudden loud noises. Although there was still a very long way to go before she was flying free, it was important that some progress was made each day, no matter how small, as it is so very easy to take one step forwards and two back. Ami was reacting well to me banging around, not appearing to be too worried. Occasionally she would bate off her perch, but she would almost immediately regain her vantage position. This was, to me a sign of progress. I had really done very little with the bird and already I could sense her relaxing more and more as each hour went by in my company. I would deliberately walk back and forth past her perching area, which was around 3 m (10 ft) from the pathway, and she would not bate. This was only her second day and I have to say I was pleasantly surprised.

That night I placed more fresh food in her weathering before putting her away. She was still bating whenever I tried picking her up, but this was not unexpected as I had not yet tempted her upon the fist.

The next three days followed more or less the same pattern, although I could now sense her acceptance whenever I walked past her on the weathering lawn or when I approached her living quarters. She was, however, still bating whenever I tried taking her up onto the fist. Her weight had now dropped to 936 g (2 lb 1 oz), as she had still not touched any food. But although she had not eaten, she was allowing me inside her aviary without bating and her general acceptance was better than I would initially have expected. I was not worried that she had not accepted any food, as her eyes were clear and wide, her keel bone was not as thin as it might be, her feathers were not at all puffed and her bates were still powerful. It was also clear that she was slowly beginning to take notice of the food which I always left beside her on the weathering lawn.

Another important thing for me was that whilst Ami was on the lawn she was becoming familiar with my chickens. Hopefully she would come to understand that chickens on a farmer's land are not potential prey and leave them well alone. I also brought the ferret run closer to her perch, so that she might learn that ferrets are also not something she ought to be killing. I hoped that she would respect the fact that they were to bolt the rabbits to which she would attempt to fly.

On the morning of the seventh day Ami's weight was recorded at 957 g (2 lb 1¾ oz). The previous night I had left a piece of rabbit in the weathering, which she had eaten. I had also removed the carpet, confident that the endless bating was almost a thing of the past. Weighing sessions were also no longer a problem. As usual I tethered her on the weathering lawn and offered her a day-old chick, which she did not accept. I left her to her own devices and went indoors. Soon after my departure, she jumped from her perch and began picking at the offering. I decided not to interrupt her, as this was the first time she had eaten away from her aviary.

Once she got going, she soon finished her meal. I could tell she wanted more so I gave her a small piece of rabbit, but this time I did not retreat. I stood about 5 m (16 ft) from her, which I am sure was intimidating. But after a while she summoned the nerve to take the offering, albeit with extreme caution.

From here on things progressed very nicely. I did not offer her any more food in her aviary; if she wanted food she would have to eat in front of me. I kept her intake to a minimum but still gave her enough to encourage her. Her weight hovered around 964 g (2 lb 2 oz).

Although Ami was slowly and surely accepting me, my chickens and my ferrets, there was another party which she might never come to accept – my black Labrador. So far she had only glimpsed the dog from a distance, and then only occasionally. Progress had so far been consistent but the full introduction of Gypsy was to be the final obstacle before I got onto the next stage of training.

To date I had not heard Ami scream, but when she first caught clear sight of Gypsy, her reaction, shall we say, was not quiet. Her bating was excessive, and when she was not bating, both her wings and mouth were as wide as wide could be. Although it is not pleasant to see a bird so scared, she would have to learn to accept the dog, as I did not intend working without a canine companion. In the case of an older Harris hawk which has never seen a dog, acceptance will be hard to achieve, if it is possible at all, but with a young bird I hoped to have less of a problem. In time I even expected her to feed next to him.

The following week showed quite a significant step toward acceptance, not only of me but also of my dog. Rarely now was she bating when I tried to pick her up, and the screaming at Gypsy thankfully seemed to be a thing of the past. Gypsy now made regular appearances, and although Ami still found him a little disturbing, she was slowly settling.

I still had not tried to handle Ami except to weigh her and to move her from the weathering lawn to the weathering. But as each day passed she was sitting on the fist a little longer, although she was still prone to the occasional bating session. By the second weekend I had decided that Ami was nicely relaxed, reasonably content with me and her new surroundings and that now would be a good time to begin the long, daunting manning process. Her weight remained around the 936 g (2 lb 1oz) mark, which I felt was a good weight to begin manning.

Manning

Although most beginners will have heard the word manning, many do not fully understand its meaning. Manning is getting the bird used to man and his environment. For example, within time, she should be at ease with your everyday life and the sudden noises which are a part of that life, such as barking dogs, sheep, cows, goats, geese, cars, lorries, tractors, people shouting, possibly planes and helicopters. In fact, she should be manned towards everything that could potentially cause upset. Impossible I hear you say, and yes, often it is. But being an optimist, I always try with every new eyass which comes into my possession.

Manning is, I believe, the most important process of the whole training programme. It is now that the falconer really gets to notice his bird, spotting markings of distinction and getting a good insight into her way of thinking. Moreover, it is the stage at which the bird begins to trust you. It is also a process which cannot be hurried. No matter what skills you may have, a nervous hawk cannot physically be made to bend her head to accept food via the gauntlet. Too many beginners underestimate the fear which a hawk experiences whilst deciding whether to bend its head to accept the first mouthful of food via the glove. Once her head goes down she can no longer see the falconer. In the wild, the bird would then be vulnerable to predators. During early manning sessions she will be getting used to you, as you are to her. She needs to be able to trust you and will not take food until she is confident and fully at ease, no matter how much she needs to feed. Birds of prey have a very long memory, and any sign of mishandling, aggression or untrustworthy behaviour as a result of impatience or frustration may never be forgotten.

Manning can often be a slow, frustrating process, with lagging progression but it must be carried out assiduously and carefully; devoting time to it will result in your bird being steadier, more reliable and less likely to stay up a tree if she catches sight of a horse or anything else which to her is alien and likely to spook her into retreat.

The first step in the manning process is to get the bird sitting comfortably upon the fist. Temperamental new arrivals after only two weeks' settling time, will no doubt bate as soon as you try to place them on the gauntlet. If this is the case put her back on. If she bates again, rescue her again. Continue like this until the bird is finally relaxed and sitting proud on the glove. Should she at any time attempt to bite your unprotected hand, lift her onto the fist from the back rather than the chest. Putting a glove on your free hand for protection is, I feel, a little over the top, and may intimidate the bird far more.

Ami was already quite relaxed upon the fist, as during the previous two weeks I had handled her quite frequently during weighing sessions and when moving her on and off the weathering lawn. I decided to go straight on to stage two, which was coaxing her to accept food via the glove. From that moment onwards, this would be her only means of getting food; no longer would she be permitted to feed on the lawn. If she chose not to eat from the fist then she would go without.

Before our initial manning session could commence, a recording of her weight was necessary; this was registered at 943 g (2 lb 1¼ oz). From this stage on, it is essential to weigh the bird at the same time every day and to record her weight in writing. Also note the volume of food consumed, as you will get to know how much a given amount of food adds to her weight.

Unlike some people, I do not do any manning or training close to a bird's living quarters, and certainly not indoors. These situations do not represent a natural environment and the lessons learnt there will be to no avail, as once she is outside, with distractions and noise, it will feel as if you are starting all over again. A bird will always progress more quickly indoors or around things which are familiar to her. The only time I break this rule is if the bird goes too long without food and begins to go under weight. The quietness of an indoor situation is more likely to get her feeding.

I placed Ami in a travelling box and drove her to a nearby field. Always take a portable seat with you for manning sessions, as standing with a bird for up to three hours or so is not very pleasant. I also take along my dog for all manning and training sessions as not only does he make an excellent foot stool, Ami must begin accepting him as a hunting partner.

On arrival at our destination, I removed Ami from the box and steadied her upon my fist while she found her footing on the glove. Once I was comfortably in my seat, I placed a piece of slashed beef in between the thumb and forefinger of the glove between Ami's feet. The idea is to wriggle the meat and tap the bird's feet simultaneously, so that she looks at the offering, and not solely at the scenic surroundings. One is lucky if the bird feeds at this juncture, as her inquisitiveness will be aroused by this novel situation.

But sitting there with Ami was time very well spent, as I was achieving something of high importance. She was getting accustomed to the environment which was to play a big part in her life. She was beginning to familiarise herself with a multitude of distractions – open spaces, birds singing, crows cawing and James the farmer, in the distance walking his trio of English springer spaniels. All these things and many more which were new to her today would on subsequent days not be so daunting. I continued wriggling the beef and gently tapping her feet, and I also began touching parts of her legs and breast, as eventually she would have to be comfortable with me handling every part of her.

After a couple of hours of intense coaxing, it was clear that she had little interest in feeding. There had been several bates, some quite severe, but she was now regaining the fist without the need for the rescuing hand, which was a very positive sign. I decided to take her and the dog for a walk around the perimeter of the field for two reasons: first to get her accustomed to riding the fist for prolonged periods, and second to relieve my aching back which after being immobilised for two hours felt very sore. This was also a good opportunity for her to see Gypsy working cover. During our walk there was the occasional bate and some raised wings, caused by the odd car which passed us as we walked alongside a lane on the other side of the field's boundary, but all in all, nothing too serious; in fact, the sight and sound of a car is all good manning. I returned to my seat and attempted every trick in the book to get her to bend her head and take a peck at the beef, but for all my efforts, it was clear that she would not be tempted. I decided to call it a day and return home. Ami was placed in her weathering with no food.

On day two, at a weight of 900 g (1 lb 15¾ oz), I once again drove Ami to the manning field. The routine was to be identical to the previous day's but, I hoped, with my goal of her accepting food achieved. With a fresh piece of slashed beef lining the glove, the coaxing and wriggling began. During the first hour, Ami hardly looked at the offering; in fact, the only time her head did go down was to bite me for touching the inside of her leg. In the second hour there was still nothing positive, so I decided to take her for another walk. This time we went through a little wooded area, into some high bramble and across a calm stream, all of which caused her no upset. Resuming my seat I tried for another hour or so but still I did not manage to get her feeding. Again she was taken home and left with no food.

Although there was little change in her weight on day three she had now gone approximately forty-eight hours without feeding. We went over to the field again to follow on from the first two days' routine. It is vital, once you have begun the manning process, that it should be completed without any break. To spend three or four days on time-consuming manning, only to let it slip, is really quite foolish. Remember, progress, no matter how small, is required daily. Repeating lessons which the bird has already learnt may be boring for her, and boredom can start a hawk screaming. Each day was different, and even though my bird was still not feeding, which is the essential goal, I was carrying out other key manning tasks, as with each session she was getting used to being with me and my dog and riding the fist. Above all, she was learning to trust me. Once I had settled her, I started wriggling the food and tapping her feet, but her thoughts appeared to be everywhere but on the gauntlet. She still refused to eat, and my final thought of the day was, perhaps tomorrow.

Overnight her weight dropped to 879 g (1 lb 15oz), but on day four, for some unknown reason I was confident that she would feed. Seventy-two hours without food must surely have made her sufficiently hungry. As each day passed I had carried out all the essential health checks, a look at her eyes and plumage and a feel of her breastbone, which was now beginning to sharpen up. The longest I had a Harris hawk go without feeding was eight days, and he was getting worryingly low in condition. Unfortunately, there is very little that one can do in these situations, except to keep encouraging the bird and allowing her the opportunity to feed every day. When she is good and ready, and only then, she will accept her first feed. Despite my optimism, however, this was not going to be that day. The only positive thing was that Ami began looking at the food more than ever before.

Whilst her eyes were still wide and her bates still strong, I was happy to continue with the pattern again on day five and as yet, there were no thoughts of bringing her indoors. It is often at this point that the beginner makes a crucial mistake. He becomes worried that his hawk has not eaten and gives her some food in the weathering. This is the sin of all sins, and you should resist all temptation to do this. If you do, all your hard work will have been wasted, and you would have rewarded your bird for something that is not positive. The whole training process is done on a food reward basis. If she does good, give her some food, but never reward her for anything which is not a positive sign of progress.

On day five, with her weight at 872 g (1 lb 14¾ oz), I tried something a little different. Instead of sitting with her immediately we reached the field, I decided to take her for a good long walk first. Perhaps if her initial curiosity was immediately satisfied, it would encourage her to feed. After our walk, I once again offered her a succulent piece of beef. Again I wriggled the food and tapped her feet, but with little effect. During the second hour, her straying gaze seemed to be more on the beef than on the scenery and I felt sure she would oblige. Suddenly she bent her head, very very cautiously, and with my gloved hand motionless her upper mandible came to rest on the beef, but there was no take. I continued to wriggle the food, and again she looked at it. Slowly her head went down and like lightning she grabbed a small piece which she immediately swallowed. Extremely cautiously, she continued to pick at the meat until the offering was finished. At last, after four and a half days, she had eaten, and from here on I envisaged things going more speedily.

It was important not to allow her too much food as progress might not be continued the following day. One has to find a happy medium: too much and you risk further progress, too little and she will not be sufficiently encouraged. From a fat aviary weight of 1014 g (2 lb 3¾ oz), she was now down to 872 g (1 lb 14¾ oz), an overall weight loss of 142 g (5 oz), 13.98 per cent of her fat aviary weight.

I was now into day six, and my next goal was to get her feeding from

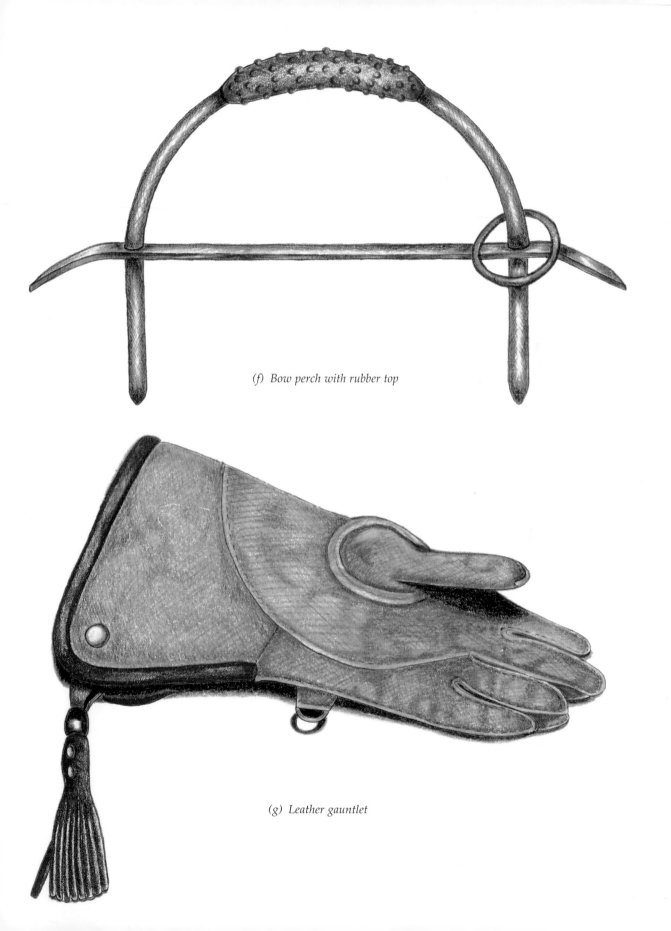

(f) Bow perch with rubber top

(g) Leather gauntlet

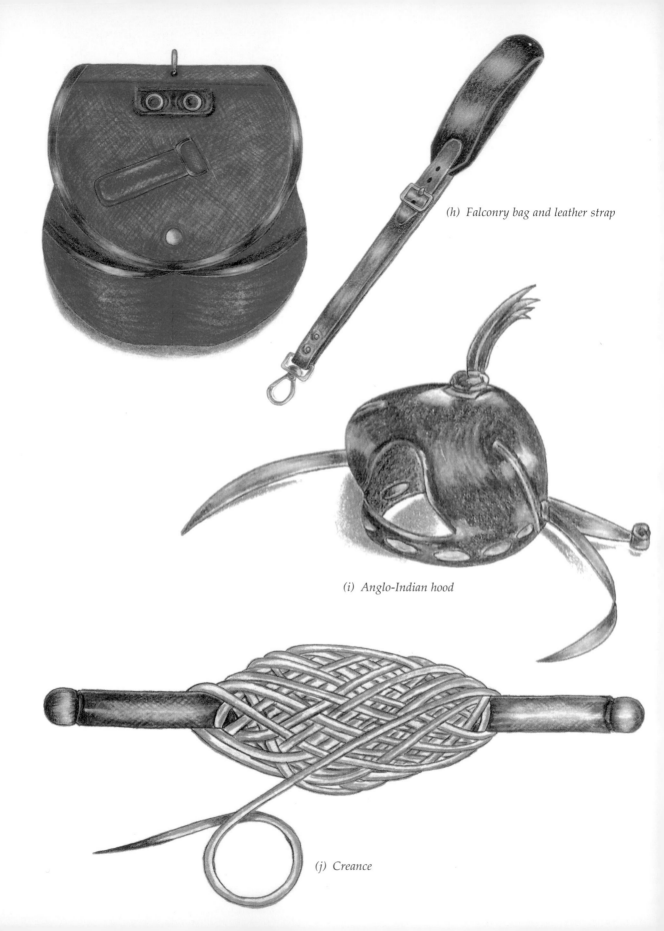

(h) Falconry bag and leather strap

(i) Anglo-Indian hood

(j) Creance

the fist as soon as food was produced. At the field once again I took Ami from the jeep and brought her onto the fist so that our walk could commence. I intended to offer her small pieces of food spontaneously throughout the course of our walk, to determine whether her desire to feed was greater than her interest in the various distractions. Initially, however, I offered her a larger piece to encourage her. Although if was not immediately accepted, she did take it without too much delay.

Our walk began. It is wise not to forget that every time you progress to another stage, it is new to the bird. Do not automatically think after ten minutes or so without her taking the food that she requires a further drop in weight; all that is likely to be required is a little more time, patience and understanding. It is at this point that some beginners start to take their birds' weight worryingly low. Should you drop a bird's weight too low, without recognising the signs which tell you this (ruffled feathers, slitty eyes, weak bates etc.), then there is every chance that she will keel over and possibly die. If, for instance, a bird is not flying to the fist on the creance it does not automatically mean that she is not hungry enough. A further drop in weight at this point could be a real threat to the bird's health whilst a gain in weight or a little extra time may see her perform. There is often more than one reason why a bird will not feed, jump to the fist or fly to the lure, so never think it is solely because she is not hungry enough. You have been warned!

So far Ami had shown no special characteristics. Like all immatures she was distracted by new objects, sounds and situations, something which would only be overcome as her weight was reduced and her curiosity was finally satisfied. She was no better or worse than the average eyass, but her strong and weak points would become more apparent during her training.

Although my goal of Ami feeding from the fist had now been achieved, this was not the end of the manning process. She had to be taking food the moment it was produced, and she had to be happy for me to touch all parts of her. It was also vital that she should accept everyday noises, as I have said. Until then, I would not move on to the next stage of her training, but I would, if necessary, devote even more of my time to her, thus keeping progress going.

At the Eagle-Owl School of Falconry we regularly take calls from worried beginners, concerned that their newly purchased Harris hawk has suddenly started to scream. They often find this hard to accept as the bird was purchased as fully parent-reared, and they expect this to be enough to guarantee her silence. If only!

A screaming hawk poses a serious problem and is a liability. In her immature year, her screams are piercing, and can continue throughout the night. They will quickly become unbearable both for you and your neighbours. A large percentage of wild-caught Harris hawks are vocal until they have completed their first major moult, so it would appear that even the best captive-bred birds are likely to be vocal.

It is often the handler's inexperience which sets his hawk off into screaming mode, as he is unable adequately to develop her natural hunting ability. So although one should never rush the training, if you do not assess your bird's daily progress, and get her on to the next stage of training and hunting as quickly as possible, she will soon become dependent on you, seeing you as the sole food provider, and it is at this point that problems are likely to arise.

During training, do not continually call the hawk to the fist; combine this with the use of both lures. If it is possible, sit the hawk next to another one whilst they are on the weathering lawn. If this is impractical, place a mirror on the weathering ground occasionally as this will remind the hawk of her identity. Never over-handle the bird or make prolonged eye contact, and do not talk to her continuously. The only vocal sounds she needs to hear and understand are the whistle commands and possibly her name.

Get your bird trained and enter her as soon as possible, or you will increase the risk of having a vocal hawk throughout her first active season, and until she is fattened up for the moult. After her moult, and once she is again cut in weight, her voice will have broken and be far less piercing, but she is unlikely to be totally silent.

Having said all that, many Harris hawks I have worked have never made a noise. Why this should be I do not know, perhaps to some extent it is luck of the draw. One year three friends each purchased a Harris hawk from the very same breeder, and from the same clutch. All were parent-reared, one male and two females, but only the male remained silent when its weight was cut. These were falconers of almost identical experience who had been flying together for many years, so the manning and training of the birds were very similar. Quite why this was, no one seems to know.

In summary, the only advice I can give on the matter of screaming is to purchase a fully parent-reared bird which is at least twenty weeks old and do not treat it in the same way as a puppy. Try to retain its identity by letting it see other hawks, stimulate its mind and get it hunting and killing as quickly as possible, and with luck you will have a youngster which remains silent.

Training

Throughout the past two weeks or so, Ami had been introduced to many distracting sights and sounds which were to a great extent now overcome, and after being bitten many times, I was now allowed to touch all parts of her torso, legs and feet. Throughout each manning session I had made a conscious effort to vary the lessons, as I did not want boredom setting in.

I had decided not to make Ami to the hood, although hood training a

Harris is simplicity itself if carried out correctly. Personally, I do not hood Harris hawks. They travel in a purpose-made wooden box and only one is taken into the field at any one time. Other falconers, however, do find hooding of benefit and should you prefer that your bird is made to the hood then it is important that it is started at the right time and that you have been taught the skills to carry it out appropriately.

Once the bird is sitting on the fist, and is comfortable there for a period of time, then hood training should commence. Do not waste your time if the bird is still temperamental and still obsessed with bating, as you will simply not succeed. Use a plain Anglo-Indian hood for a Harris hawk; this is the best-fitting for the species, and if you are inexperienced, it is far easier to slip over the head than the Dutch blocked hoods, for instance. A week or so before the bird is to be picked up from the breeder, you should ask him if he has any idea of its eventual flying weight. Breeders will often have an good idea from previous years' offspring from the same parentage. Telephone your equipment supplier and order a hood, giving the hawk's gender and approximate flying weight. If you have a good relationship with your supplier you may find that the company is prepared to send you two or three to try. When your bird is initially cast for equipping, place the hood over the head, draw the braces and check it for fit. If it is wrong, send it back and get the appropriate size. Never use a hood which does not fit perfectly. The fundamentals of correct hooding should be taught on a well-structured course.

Throughout the latter part of the manning sessions, Ami's weight remained consistent at around 879 g (1 lb 15 oz). She was responding well to all lessons and appeared manageable and keen, so I held her around this weight, as I felt it was the right time to proceed to the next stage of training, which was getting her to step up onto the fist for a reward.

During all the previous manning sessions the weather had been kind, with no wind and no rain, but when I arrived at the training ground that day there was a wind that was little less than gale force. This could have a dire effect on progress, as such an extreme wind was something alien to the bird. Not wanting to jeopardise progress at this early stage, I found a little secluded area which offered us some protection.

Although many beginners do not see the point of asking a bird to step up onto the fist, this little lesson is extremely helpful in the weathering, in getting the bird onto the fist with minimal fuss. Whilst she is busy nibbling on a chick leg, you are able to untie the leash and promptly leave, thus minimising the risk of feather damage occurring should she spontaneously bate in such a confined area. It is also beneficial when taking the bird up onto the fist after she has killed or come down to the lure. Never underestimate this important lesson, which should always be taught as part of the training process.

It is important to face an immature bird into the wind during stepping-up lessons, and even more important when she is on the creance and flying at longer ranges, as having the wind behind her will affect her co-ordination, which could result in her overshooting the fist and heading straight for the nearest tree – something one tries to avoid.

To get a hawk stepping onto the fist, one should garnish one's glove well. As always, Ami was given an initial mouthful of food via the glove to encourage her and to show me that she was indeed ready to feed. With the bird sitting on the perch, gently push a garnished glove at the point where the flank feathers end. The idea is that she should step onto the fist for the reward, but it will rarely be this simple. It is more common for her to stretch out or bend her neck in a desperate bid to steal the offering. Do not let her succeed in doing this. Harris hawks are excellent opportunists and I have been caught out on many occasions. If she tries, slowly move the glove away from her. Frustrated, she may well try to hold the offering steady with a foot. If she does, slowly lift the glove where it is intended she places the other foot on. If she does so, allow her the reward. If she does not, continue the same process.

Stepping onto the fist was something Ami took to both quickly and positively, and once this lesson was truly mastered, I spent time just placing her on and off her perch. Every now and again, she would be given a reward in the form of a piece of rabbit. She was then asked to hop onto the fist, which is the very next stage in the training process. It is at this point

(21) Ami stepping onto the fist

that the bird begins to understand that the offering of food upon the glove, accompanied by a blast on the whistle, means that she should return to her handler.

Once she was settled on her perch, I placed a lean piece of beef in the glove. From a distance of approximately 1 m (3 ft 3 in) the full length of the leash, I gave the glove a tap with my ungloved hand, accompanied by a sharp, short blast on the whistle. Ami's eyes were glued on the offering. I tend to remain kneeling at this point as to crowd a bird from such a short distance could make her feel intimidated. It was clear she wanted to feed, but there was no immediate reaction. I relentlessly wriggled the beef and tapped the glove, blowing the whistle as I did so, but this was something new to her and would actually be her first ever move towards me. Before long, however, her concentration started to stray until eventually I was unable to get her focusing on the reward at all. After approximately ninety minutes, it was clear that she was not going to jump, so she was taken home and left overnight without any food.

The following day there was a reduction in the fierce wind and the weather was again bright and mild. Ami weighed in at 865 g (1 lb 14½ oz). Once on the training field, and after her usual mouthful upon the fist, Ami was positioned on the perch to face the light breeze. An offering of fresh beef was placed on the glove and the coaxing began. Within minutes she had found the nerve to jump onto the fist, but she instantly turned around and jumped back to her perch. Moments later, she again made a worried jump onto the fist, but this time she found her footing on the glove, had a quick look around and accepted the offering. A bird will often fly onto the glove, attempt to grab the food and take it back to the perch. She should not be allowed to do this, so be careful and hold the offering tightly.

After a few further attempts Ami was hopping to me the short distance of a full leash length with very little hesitation. The next stage was to remove the leash and attach the creance. At this stage I stood to call the bird. From a distance of approximately 5 m (16 ft 3 in), I called Ami to the fist with the whistle command. She was instantly at me. I was a little surprised at her quick response, as this was the first time I had stood tall to call her.

A word of warning regarding the safe use of the creance. Make sure the ground you are training over is smooth so that the thin line does not snag, as this may add unnecessary stress to the bird's legs. It is important that the handle is placed in the falconry bag or is securely under a foot; if the hawk overshoots the fist you do not want her snagged up within a tree. Obviously the line must not have any weak areas which could snap under pressure, as a semi-trained bird flying loose with trailing line is major cause for concern.

As always, progress through the training as quickly as your bird will allow but never go from leash length to full creance length; build the distance up gradually or you risk stopping progress altogether, as your

(22) Ami on the creance

bird may simply lose her nerve if she is asked to do too much too quickly. And never stand immediately in front of an enticing tree, as she might overshoot the fist and try to settle there, and you will have no alternative but to pull her up by tautening the line which, as I have already said, can cause discomfort to the legs.

Suppliers of falconry equipment will sell the creance with different lengths of line, normally 25 or 50 m. I have seen some beginners with what appears to be a mile of line. This is a sign that he is worried about actually flying her free. But you cannot enjoy falconry and witness the spectacular flight ability of your bird if she is restricted to a training line. In my opinion if a bird is confidently coming to the fist at 25 m then I am pretty sure she will come at 50 m, but slowly slowly should be the order of the day.

By the end of Ami's first session on the creance, she was flying the full 25 m. Not once did she overshoot the fist, and I decided that was enough as I wanted to introduce her to the rabbit lure the following day, so an increase in her weight would not be a good idea.

The first sight of the rabbit lure can often be daunting to a young hawk.

To minimise her fear, I believe the easiest way to introduce this item is to tie it in the weathering, garnished with a good-sized reward, and to leave the bird to it overnight. It is important that the lure is securely tacked to the bottom of the weathering so that the hawk cannot carry it to the perch, as carrying smaller kills to a high perch in the field is a frustratingly bad habit. That evening I cut a length of creance line, approximately 45 cm (18 in) long, and fastened one end securely to the lure and the other to the weathering panel. It was garnished well with washed rabbit, as this would not affect her weight too much.

The following morning the food had been taken and Ami had been introduced to the lure in her own time and with minimal fuss. She was immediately offered a pick-up piece and taken into the weighing room. Her weight was recorded at 872 g (1 lb 14¾ oz). She had cast a pellet overnight, indicating that her stomach was empty and she should be ready to feed.

Harris hawks can be introduced to both the rabbit and the swing lure, but it is preferable to show only one at a time. The other can be introduced when the bird is confident with the first. Although I prefer to begin with the rabbit lure there are no hard and fast rules to this; it was just that Ami's first kill was likely to be fur. Before Ami was allowed to see the rabbit lure in the field, I gave her a quick recap of the lessons learnt so far – a mouthful of food whilst on the glove, a few flights on the creance and some stepping up and putting down on the bow. When you are ready, and with the bird on the fist, tie a full leash length to the tethering ring and place her on the perch. Do not swing the rabbit lure and do not ask her to fly too far for it. Garnish it well – again I use washed rabbit – and place it to the side of the perch at a distance of approximately 60 cm (2 ft). Ami's first response was identical to that of many other hawks I have trained, to bate in the opposite direction. If this happens, put the lure away and place the bird back on the perch. Give her a minute or so to settle and repeat the exercise. After a few further bates in the opposite direction, Ami at last decided to sit still. To direct a bird's attention towards the lure, gently tug the line so that it makes short, sharp movements. Ami was quite alarmed by this and it was clear after some time that she was not going to jump to it.

Although little had been achieved in that session I was reluctant to drop her weight further, as it was still early days. Instead I took her home, leaving the lure beside her ungarnished, and returned in the evening when there was more chance of her succeeding. She clearly wanted to feed, but she was just a little nervy. If she did not perform later on then again she would go without food.

That evening I took her back to the training field. Although her weight was the same as it was in the morning she had now gone approximately six hours more without food. With the leash tied to the tethering ring, I again placed the lure to the side of her. After a few twitches of the line, she hopped from the perch and walked over towards the food. But showing her opportunist traits, instead of standing on the lure's body, she attempted to steal a mouthful by extending her neck. This again is something that a bird should not get away with. Instead, pull the lure towards you; the intention is that she throws out a foot to hold it still. If she does, continue pulling the line until she brings the other foot on. Ami, however, did things slightly different. She attempted to grab the lure, by extending her neck, so I pulled the line. She did not thrust out a foot, however; instead, she flew back to her perch. Again I carried out the same routine, and again she flew to the side of the lure and extended her neck, so I gently pulled the lure from her. Although she did not fly back to her perch this time, she did not attempt to hold it steady. Instead she continued walking towards it until she had come to the end of the leash length. Ami was placed back on her perch and I tried once again. This time she actually flew onto the lure, but with only one foot on the body. I gently pulled the line and she quickly placed the other foot on. I immediately let her feed. By the end of the session, she had still not left her perch and hit the lure with both feet, but progress had been made and I now had something positive to work on.

The following day Ami had dropped 7 g (¼ oz) in weight to 865 g (1 lb 14½ oz), partly due to her diet of late consisting of washed rabbit, and also the fact that she had had very little to eat within the last twenty-four hours. Although this slight reduction in weight was neither intended nor required as I was pretty certain that she would hit the lure directly at 872 g (1 lb 14¾ oz), and probably even a bit higher given a little more time, it was going to take me a long time to understand her metabolism, so unintentional mistakes were bound to occur – certainly at this early stage and probably throughout her first year.

Back at the training field, a quick offering upon the fist was given before Ami was tethered to the perch. The lure was garnished well and placed to the side of her approximately 1 m (3 ft 3 in) away. She instantly focused on it, bobbed her head a few times and flew to its side. I pulled the lure from her and a foot was instantly thrust out to hold it steady. I continued to pull the lure until her other foot come to rest upon it. I then allowed her to feed. Again she was placed on her perch and the routine repeated. With each flight a little more aggression was shown but still she did not hit the lure full on with both feet.

I knew if she did it just once, she would no doubt continue to do it. And by the end of a very long session, she was hitting the lure directly with both feet, although tentatively. The following day I would be swapping the leash for the creance, hoping she would begin flying further distances for her reward. Once she was flying approximately 12 m (39 ft) or so, I would start to make in on her. Making in is an essential part of lure training. It basically involves swapping captured quarry, or during training the lure, for an offering upon the glove. This obviously simulates a true-to-life situation in the field.

With Ami now on the creance, things could become a little awkward, especially as the line got longer. Not only is it very easy for the creance and lure lines to cross, which can leave one in a terrible mess, more importantly the bird might overshoot, so again extend the creance line by sensible lengths.

Initially I asked Ami to fly a distance of 3 m (10 ft) to the rabbit lure. This she did, hitting it directly with both feet, which was a welcome surprise. The creance was then extended to 6 m (20 ft) and then to 9 m (30 ft). Each time, she hit it correctly she was rewarded, and rewarded well. This did mean, however, that her weight would go up far more quickly than if the lure had been garnished with a single chick leg. But during these early stages the bird must be rewarded heavily, to give a chick leg is not much of an incentive and could even discourage the bird.

By the end of this session Ami was flying approximately 9 m (30 ft) to the lure before she began to slow. Her flights had been instantaneous, often before I had time to blow the whistle. She had learnt a great deal overnight, or so it appeared, but such is the intelligence of the Harris hawk that they normally do. Occasionally I alternated the routine by asking her to fly to the fist, which made the session fractionally more interesting. I decided to call it a day at this point and return the following day, when my goal of getting her to fly the full length of the creance and of making in on her would hopefully be achieved.

Ami's weight the following morning was recorded at 865 g (1lb 14½ oz). Once she had had her normal piece of meat upon the glove, the leash was replaced by the creance and extended to 9 m (30 ft). The rabbit lure was taken from my bag and dropped to my side. As it hit the floor Ami was in

23) Making in

flight, hitting the head end with what appeared to be real aggression. This routine was repeated a few more times, then the line was extended to 12 m (39 ft). On this flight I wanted to attempt to make in on her and swap the lure for a pick-up piece on the glove. It is at this point that the stepping-up lessons are of benefit. Initially the bird will be reluctant to step from the lure onto the glove for a reward, which in her eyes may not be fair.

Ami flew onto the lure as soon as it hit the ground. Whilst she was accepting her reward, I crouched down on all fours, gloved arm extended with food, and crawled in towards her. As I approached, her gaze was on the glove, as she had consumed the food which I had secured to the lure. I put my hawking bag over the lure and placed the gauntlet at the point just above her flank feathers. She stepped on, although she was reluctant to drop the lure. I then allowed her the offering on the glove.

When your bird makes a kill for real, you should cover the quarry with a towel or your falconry bag whilst the bird is on it, and throw some food to the side. This gives you the opportunity to dispatch the animal quickly whilst the bird is busy feeding on the tit-bits.

By the end of the day Ami was flying the full 25 m of the creance, both to the fist and to the lure. The next day, weather permitting, I would be flying her free for the first time. This was an exciting time, as I could now work on her fitness and at last begin thinking of entering.

Ninety per cent of beginners are very concerned about flying their hawks free for the first time. Provided you have carried out both the manning and training processes correctly, however, you have little to worry about. Using telemetry will obviously give you peace of mind and help calm your nerves. However, do not rush to get your charge flying free, and only loose her when you are totally happy, not because others are putting pressure on you. You should know your bird better than anybody else and deep down you will know when the time is right.

The following day was thankfully still, a great day to set a hawk loose for the first time. Initially I gave Ami a few flights on the creance fully extended before taking off her swivel and attaching flying jesses. Never fly a bird free with mews jesses, as these could easily get caught up if the bird goes into a tree. I fixed a transmitter to the tail mount, which was already in place, and I was ready.

Her first flight was from a low branch at a distance of approximately 15 m. Ami had never been in a tree before so I did not expect any immediate flight. However, I called her to the fist and she was at me with very little hesitation. I placed her back on the same branch for her second flight but thereafter varied the perching positions to make this first free-flying lesson simple but exciting. Although I would begin casting her into trees the following day, I would be calling her straight back to the fist. During her first season all slips at quarry would be from the fist. I did not want her chasing from trees and I would not be asking her to follow on. Nothing which might encourage her to self-hunt would be done at this influential stage. However, I did not want her feeling intimidated by being amongst trees; if a slip should result in a miss and she ended up there, I would want her back to the fist quickly. After a season of fist work, she would be somewhat experienced and during her second season I would get her to follow on, but for the time being, it was fist work only, which in my opinion produces far better flights.

After a hour or so, Ami was beginning to tire and slow up. Her work ratio had been greater than ever before and at that point work stopped. During this session she flew to the fist only. The next day I would be combining this with the use of the lure.

A word of warning: as the bird begins to do more work, so more body fat and energy will be used. This has to be replaced with extra rations (the food to work ratio). If it is not, the hawk will soon start to go weak.

The following day saw the wind picking up once again. As I have said, it is vital that all flights to the fist or lure are with her facing into the wind. With her weight slightly up at 872 g (1 lb 14¾ oz), Ami was, for the very first time, cast from the fist in the direction of a dead oak which had lovely, inviting branches. She did not land on the branch I intended; instead she flew to the very highest point, which I thought would slow her response back to the fist. A quick offering of food and a blast on the whistle made her take to the wing and glide onto the fist, showing a slow controlled flight. I cast her again and this time she settled on a lower branch. I took out the rabbit lure and dropped it to the ground. She looked at it. I twitched the line and she looked at it harder. I twitched it once more and she took to the wing, hitting the lure head-on in fine fashion.

During the next few days these lessons were repeated, and I also started running with the lure as soon as it hit the ground. I also introduced the swing lure, and she began doing jump-ups, which is flying from the ground vertically onto the fist. This takes a lot of effort and really gets the wings pumping. Start doing these once your bird is flying free, do not ask her to do too many and build the number up daily. They will build muscle and help get her flying fit for the field.

After a week of flying free, both to the fist and to lures, and after an increasing number of jump-ups daily, Ami was as fit as she could possibly be at this stage. The only way she would attain full physical fitness was to chase quarry. Like all immature birds, she would require a kill quickly and from the easiest of slips, as she could get disheartened if prey constantly eluded her. My next task, therefore, was to get her entered.

Entering

It is necessary that the falconer entering his juvenile hawk should be *field organised*, as this will help her tremendously to make her first and subsequent few kills. It is important that tried and trusted land is used so that the easiest of slips are presented to the bird. You should know the lie of the trees, those which are in fuller leaf and those which are bare, as bare branches are easier for a hawk to enter and leave should quarry get up. Bare trees also make it easier for the hawk to spot bolting quarry. Understand the lie of the hedgerows and what quarry frequents them. Locate burrows, and the places where rabbits lay up. Rabbits are not stupid; they have excellent hearing and eyesight, and a good sense of smell and vibration, and will warn each over of approaching danger by thumping their hind feet against the ground. Respect the rabbit and understand its biology, feeding and behavioural traits or you will not succeed. All these things are vitally important and could make the difference between a kill or an empty bag.

To date Ami had done me proud. She was a lovely-natured bird who had been quick to learn. I had put a great deal of time and effort into her training and well-being and I now wanted to reap my rewards. Come September I, like all falconers, get itchy feet. The hawking season always seems to be a long time coming around, and Ami had reached the stage when the only thing on my mind was to get out hunting. With an eyass of the year, which at this stage still has a lot more to learn, it is vital that she is entered as early on in the season as possible. Younger, more vulnerable rabbits will be about and their vulnerability could benefit the bird.

On Ami's first day out in search of quarry, I took her to a tried and trusted piece of land. For now I would not be casting her into trees and beating below her; instead, I would be beating whilst she was on the fist. Thankfully the weather was mild and it was not windy. Pick a calm day to enter your hawk as this will make her task easier. Before I left home, Ami was weighed at 850 g (1 lb 14 oz), and I made absolutely sure that she had cast a pellet or she would not have had the desire to feed. The previous day she had been given half her normal ration, as the intention was to sharpen her up just a little more. Arriving at our destination, the first thing I did was to attach a transmitter to her tail mount and check that it was working and that the signal was strong. I then removed her mews jesses and attached flyers before she was offered half a chick leg on the fist to whet her appetite and to make sure she was willing to feed. Before a hawk is taken into the field it is essential that she is in fine health. Always carry out the daily health checks, taking note of her faeces and making sure she has cast a pellet before leaving for the field, otherwise you risk her loss or her misbehaving.

I walked her to the start of a very long hedgerow which I knew could spontaneously produce a moorhen, woodcock or rabbit. As we walked, I began beating the cover, using my trusted stick. Waving and crunching a long stick can be extremely daunting behaviour to a young hawk so make sure she is fully relaxed with this before you begin. It is often wise to introduce this style of quarry flushing during manning and training sessions, preferably when she is taken for her walks upon the fist. A wood pigeon got up. Ami saw it and took flight, but she had little chance of a kill, so she pulled up and took shelter in the nearest tree. Before I had time to recall her a rabbit bolted and sprinted rapidly along semi-thick covert. I looked at Ami, who was focused strongly on the rabbit as if admiring its agility but she did little more than watch it run to safety. With nothing worth cheering about I called her back to the fist and gave her half a chick leg. One always hopes that the bird will take to the wing as soon as quarry is spotted but this is not always the case. Entering can be extremely frustrating. The bird, although enthusiastic on both lures may not give live sport a second glance. This could be because she does not see the quarry till late or else because of lack of fitness. Although their vision is far superior to our own, they often appear not to a notice a rabbit breaking cover when we mere mortals have seen it perfectly clearly. Fitness and self-belief can also play their part. Unfortunately all one can do is continually look for easy openings, and eventually it will come.

With Ami back on the fist, we continued our walk along the hedge. Something caught her eye, and she bated, but I held her back as I was not sure whether it was just a naughty bate or whether in fact she wanted to

(24) Beating a hedgerow

fly something. Normally I would have let her go but on the spur of the moment I stopped her. By the time we had reached the end of the hedgerow nothing else had broken so I walked Ami into some woodland after stopping off at my vehicle to pick up Gypsy, my Labrador.

Although there was every chance that a rabbit would bolt, there was, in that sort of terrain, also the risk that Ami would spot a squirrel. Should she be loose at the time, then she might have attempted her first kill on prey which can give a nasty bite. Although I enjoy squirrel hawking, and part of the reason for purchasing Ami was to do some, I wanted her to build up her fitness, and stamina and attain better, faster reflexes before she attempted quarry which can potentially do a complacent hawk severe damage.

Our time following Gypsy was time well spent as a rabbit got up and began its run to safety. Ami instantly spotted it and left the fist in pumping pursuit. The rabbit hit cover and Ami, unlike a redtail, refused to hit the dense overgrowth, being happier to sit on a branch directly above. I

(25) Gypsy working woodland

sent Gypsy in to attempt a reflush, but before he got there Ami had stooped from the tree and the chase continued. Although I ran as fast as I could, it was the start of the season and like Ami I was also short of stamina, and I lost sight of her as she went over and down an undulation. I eventually found her, or heard her bells; she was sitting on an open branch surveying the cover immediately below her. I called her back to the fist so that we could both enjoy a much-needed rest.

The remainder of the day provided little else in terms of bolting quarry so to end the session, Ami was made to chase the rabbit lure for her daily ration. Although I had not got her a kill, I left the field feeling optimistic as, after her initial reluctance to chase quarry, she quickly began flying with some enthusiasm, indicating that her killing weight was pretty much correct. I knew she would connect, it was just a matter of time.

On day two of our pursuit of a kill, with no overnight change in her weight, I took Ami to the same venue, but we walked a different section. A large field offered us rough ground. Although this is, in my opinion, the best terrain to slip from the fist, as one almost always gets to see the whole chase, every twist and turn and even the end result, it can make the spotting of quarry difficult for the hawk. However, I was sure we would put up some rabbits so we entered. I had walked no more than 3 m (10 ft) into the field when a rabbit bolted. Ami instantly left the fist, hit and bound her target backside on, only to lose her footing and thus her first kill. It is always preferable for the bird to hit the quarry on the head, as we teach them during lure training, but this is not the lure, it is not a simulated situation, this is the real thing and the bird has to learn, as it will, that by hitting the head there is more chance of stopping the prey. Also, a bird which is *able footed* will, in time, still keep hold of the quarry, even if it hits its hind end. Those which do not use their feet optimally will miss kills time after time, some even when the quarry has been hit correctly. The only way to correct this is by additional rabbit-lure training. Whilst the bird is on the lure try and simulate a struggling rabbit. If you are able to get the lure away from the bird with reasonable ease, then in the field the rabbit would probably have got away.

Now Ami was flying quarry my major concern was that she should bind onto something quickly. Otherwise I might risk her not chasing at all, as with each miss self-doubts would begin plaguing her mind. Although this was only her second day out, this dilemma was firmly in my mind. In the wild a hawk will die if it does not kill. In captivity, a hunting hawk which does not kill still gets food. Why then should she waste a lot of energy trying to connect when she still gets fed? This is the way a raptor thinks, why do something for nothing? Not until she has killed and been allowed a full crop will she be motivated to use her energy to the full, as her hard work will then have been rewarded.

After her hit and miss, Ami was now back on the fist, and frantically looking around as if knowing that a potential meal could bolt at any time.

Again a rabbit got up and again she left the fist. I sensed more speed in her flight, as if she knew the rabbit would disappear at any moment, her wings relentlessly pumping and her enthusiasm seemingly still high. Her target, however, was both quick and experienced and wasted no time hitting thick cover. Ami had tried her damnedest but was left pondering as she sat on the ground, catching her breath. She was tiring by this time; two chases on top of each other had certainly taken their toll.

The field we were in was alive with rabbits and I knew that one was certain to get up at any time. What I did not want was for Ami to attempt to chase when she was tired, as this would only add to her day's disappointment. I decided to sit with her and allow her a few mouthfuls of meat whilst she was on the fist and regaining her breath. Once I felt she was ready we continued our pursuit. I love this style of hawking: it is so exciting, especially with a bird which is experienced and flying fit. The pulse is racing continuously, as rapid action can commence at any time. Again a rabbit took to its feet, and Ami was there, refreshed and eager. She hit it towards the head, tumbling as she did, but this time she managed to keep locked on. I sensed that the target was not too big, so by using her large, powerful feet correctly I was sure that this was to be her first success. It was. I raced over. The rabbit was still alive, wriggling and trying to elude her, but there was little chance of that. I went in and dispatched the rabbit quickly and cleanly. I made an incision along the neck, being extremely careful that the blade did not come into contact with the bird's feet. I then stood off and let Ami tuck in; she had certainly earned it.

Many things were running through my head as I watched her enjoy her first kill: the day I gave Paul Harris my deposit, the day she arrived home, the settling-in period, the manning, the training, the extra work I had put in to keep progress going, all for this moment. Here we were, her first kill taken in reasonable style from the fist, over good sporting terrain against a rabbit in healthy condition – two athletes in competition but with only one winner. I had managed to view her first kill from start to finish and her flight, although a little untidy, was powerful, and given time it would be methodical. The time and money that I had spent on her had all been worth it, for I had at last reaped the rewards of my hard work and dedication, and once again this unrivalled sport had brought me closer to nature as no other could possibly do.

Like all broadwings and shortwings, Ami was allowed to feed up slightly on her kill on the ground before I brought her up onto the fist to indulge in a full crop. It was not wise to fly her again that day for obvious reasons: she would be overweight. I tend to follow the same pattern for the bird's first five or six kills. One kill per outing during this period is ample, and it is vital that after each kill she should be given a good portion to feed on, as this gives encouragement. Should you begin robbing your bird, taking kills off her the moment they have been dispatched just so that you can continue hawking, then you risk losing her motivation until she perhaps declines to kill altogether. Even in the wild a bird of prey would not be continually robbed by competitors.

After her first half-dozen head or so, you can start taking captured quarry from her, although she ought to be given a reward after every success and a full crop once a week. This way one can enjoy all day hawking without ever jeopardising her performance.

Once an eyass has made her first kill and been heavily rewarded, she should go from strength to strength. Nothing encourages like success so it is important to continue giving the bird easy slips for her first five or six kills, as she will still be very much learning. But during this delicate period she will be achieving and maintaining full fitness, so harder slips can slowly be introduced. It is at this point that the versatility of the bird becomes apparent.

Approximately one month after entering Ami, she had six heads firmly behind her – four rabbits and two moorhen. Because she had been rewarded well after each kill, I was unable to fly her every day, as she was regularly over hunting weight. Day by day she was improving and showing signs of making a good hunting hawk. I had introduced her to some trickier flights, which did not put her off as the result was two kills taken in fine style.

Although all suitably trained and experienced hawks will kill, not all will hunt. A good, intelligent hunting Harris will understand the lie of the land and how to use it to her advantage. She will understand what the dog, ferret and beaters are doing, and will normally fly successfully in a cast (as a pair). But these skills will rarely be seen in a weekender's bird. It is the falconer who works his bird hard, giving her the time required to get her trained, flying and chasing quarry, who will see his bird reach her true potential.

Now that Ami was killing, I could begin thinking of field meetings. Personally I like my birds to be as fit as I can possibly get them before I go to field meetings, as they will be working in full view of others. I owe it to them to ensure that they are able to give a good account of themselves. I believed I was nearing this stage with Ami. All that was left for me to do was work her alongside the ferrets and over a few different dogs. When I was confident that she would not kill a ferret I would attend the first field meeting.

Ferrets are worth their weight in gold. Whilst some falconers are lucky enough to have an abundance of rabbits, others will not be so spoilt and ferreting may be the only way of giving a bird a flight. Not all warrens will produce suitable quarry. If they are too large, the rabbits may appear briefly from one hole before shooting straight down another. If they are too close to the covert then the rabbits will simply run to immediate safety. Ideally a warren ought to be away from cover and on a slope so that bolting rabbits run downhill which gives the hawk additional speed.

(26) Placing a ferret into a warren

Ferreting must be taken extremely seriously if you are to have any success, but when everything comes together then it is one of the most quick-fired, blood-rushing ways to fly a bird of prey.

Attending field meetings

Field meetings, whether organised by a club or by a group of friends, should be taken extremely seriously. For some, this weekend entertainment is time to be treasured, owing to work pressures during the week. For others, it is a time to meet up with friends and enjoy quality companionship. Although I am privileged to be able to go out hawking every day throughout the season, it can occasionally became a little lonely, as friends and associates are busy with work commitments. For me, therefore, meets, whether large or small, are refreshing. I can spend valuable time with other falconers and see other birds flying. Field meetings also give one the chance to exhibit one's bird. Hopefully the bird will give a good account of herself and the other attendees are able to see that she has been trained in a professional way. It is important that the hawk is familiar with quarry and fit enough to attempt a kill. She should obviously be at a correct hunting weight, healthy and strong.

No matter how well a bird is trained, however, it takes many, many

(27) Ami and me
attending our first
field meet

outings before one has a competent hawk. I believe it takes at least two to three full seasons to produce a bird to be proud of. Throughout this period one must be dedicated to the bird, ironing out misdemeanours before they have a chance to settle. The more she is flown the better she will become. Lazy falconers produce lazy birds and lazy birds will not make competent falconry birds. It is a vicious circle which can only be broken by those who truly love their sport. I have known beginners who, through a lack of knowledge, experience and understanding, have expected too much from their charges. They see a fit flying bird making regular kills from the hardest of slips and wonder why their birds are not doing the same. An eyass of the year needs nurturing and bringing on, she depends on your ability and she requires your time. Patience is vital but so too is the knowledge to take her successfully through the manning, training and entering without making irreversible mistakes. Understanding falconry and the particular species one is working with is a basic requirement, and if you do not have that understanding, then you are in severe trouble, and you should not have a bird such as this. All too often I see badly trained birds which, when not self-hunting or sitting in a tree refusing to come back to the fist, do little else than scream, whose owners are quite content to blame everything other than their own inability.

Although the odd field meet will always be overshadowed by a falconry bigot or two, those who truly understand the sport will quite clearly know the difference between a bird which has been well trained but is still learning her trade, and one which has been handled by someone whose very right to own a raptor is open to question. Field meetings should be enjoyed, there is no room for the falconer who takes a 'my bird is better than yours' attitude.

They are also a way to further one's own knowledge and a chance to talk falconry with falconry people and to enjoy watching different species go about their business in various ways.

Field meeting – Suffolk

Ami's first organised meet of the season was towards the end of November with two other Harris hawks, both like Ami in their first season, and one redtail which was in his fourth. Towards the end of the previous season, someone I knew had been granted permission on approximately 400 ha (1000 acres) of arable land which had clusters of picturesque woodland on its outskirts. I was itching to get into this woodland as Ami had shown a real aptitude in this terrain and it was here that I felt most confident. The four of us had been looking forward to this meet for many months, as on our pre-season visits quarry had been in abundance.

Setting off at first light, the weather was, to say the least, unpredictable, although the skies had cheered up somewhat when we arrived at our destination. The birds were taken from their travelling boxes and tethered to bows. Names were put into a hat and, as always, mine was the last to be drawn. This meant that depending on the amount of quarry, Ami could have a long time to wait for a flight. Once the birds were fitted with tags and appropriate jesses, we went off. Gypsy, my Labrador and Jo, a German short-haired pointer were the dogs for today and poor old Jim, our faithful beater, was once again lumbered with holding the ferret boxes, digging spade, binoculars and telemetry cases. The land was very sandy, with confirmed warrens in the middle of wide open spaces. This meant that bolting rabbits had a very long run to cover. A polecat was carefully placed in an inviting warren and the two other Harris hawks were to have first and second slips. These two birds had had many outings together and could be trusted loose at the same time. A rabbit bolted and the first male Harris gave chase. Another rabbit appeared and the second Harris was set free. Both birds were hot in the pursuit, with Ami and the male redtail looking on, both bating, frantically trying to take flight, but both were held back. The first Harris hawk bound onto its target, hitting it head-on with precision, the second missed but only just.

The next slip was Bob's male redtail, Sandy. His pointer, Jo, was allowed her head and took wind to something in semi-covert. The redtail was placed above the dog to take up a vantage point within a tree. A rabbit broke and began its run along the edge of semi-thick rough but the redtail was with it, a bird of many seasons' experience and an immensely powerful bird with a good hunting brain. The rabbit side-kicked into bramble, but the bird followed, crashing into a mass of uninviting cover, but the chase was over. The rabbit had escaped leaving Bob the job of carefully unwrapping his still fighting bird from the thick mass of cover.

Next it was Ami's chance. Gypsy began working a hedgerow but Jim, our beater, had noticed a nice warren and halted proceedings. A ferret was placed into the warren and all went silent. Through lack of experience, Ami is not fully focused on a warren when a ferret is placed within it. A seasoned hawk will sit on the fist erect, looking and waiting for something to bolt, understanding the role of the ferret. Once an immature hawk takes a few rabbits in this way, she too will start being fully focused.

Soon a rabbit bolted. Ami left the fist, charged up and beating her wings hard. The rabbit twisted and turned, hopped and jumped, but Ami was with him. She thrust out a foot, but her attack was cleverly dodged. She regained her momentum in time to follow her target behind some bramble, and I heard a scream which told me the chase was over. Ami had both her massive feet tightly on the head, which was an encouraging sight. The rabbit was quickly dispatched and the neck opened so that she could take her well-deserved reward. The weather by this time had turned cloudy and I knew our day would be cut short, so I allowed her a good cropful.

All in all, apart from, the weather, it had been a good day. All the birds flew well and apart from Bob's redtail, all eventually made a kill.

Field meeting – Essex

How very refreshing it is to go hawking when the venue is close to one's own home. Harlow harbours many falconers, so land is very hard to come by. A friend of mine, however, is friendly with a local farmer who was suffering a heavy rabbit infestation on his 320 ha (800 acres).

It was mid January and this was a day which for me was best forgotten. Something had upset Ami. From the moment she was taken from the travelling box she began bating. This in itself was unusual, but even more displeasing was her reluctance to regain the fist. I had a feeling that she would play me up, and she did. As we walked towards the field, she consistently bated. I really could not understand what was wrong. She had the desire to feed as she bated frantically towards my ungloved hand whenever food was produced. I really was puzzled. We entered the field, and a rabbit got up so I slipped her. Although she flew well, she missed her target and came to rest within a tree. I immediately pulled out a recall piece of meat, which she totally ignored. I exchanged this small piece for a full chick but still she seemed determined to make me look a fool. I could not think of any change to her normal pattern within the last twenty-four hours to account for this behaviour. I had changed one anklet the night before as the leather had begun to curl, but surely this unruly behaviour could not be because of that. I got Bob to call her whilst I held his bird. He placed a chick on his glove and whistled, and Ami left the tree. She flew to him and attempted to grab the chick from the gauntlet. She did not succeed and went back to rest in the tree. How glad I was that I had not travelled miles for this.

I told the others to carry on without me and in sheer desperation I tied a chick to a pad, swung it a few times, and let it hit the ground. Ami obliged by flying down to it immediately. Whilst she was busy eating, I made in. I crouched down on all fours, afraid that she may leave her meal to retire to a tree once again. She did not. I grabbed her jesses and took her straight back to the car.

Here was a bird which was fully manned, fully at ease with me and most things which went on around her, a bird in fine health, and at a correct flying weight of 879 g (1 lb 15oz), a bird that was normally very obedient, and very trustworthy. I could only put her misbehaviour down to my casting her the evening before. Nothing else had been any different to the norm.

After finishing the day beating for the rest of the lads, I took Ami home and allowed her a full crop via the fist. I had to win her trust back and this was the only way I knew of doing it.

Field meeting – Bedfordshire

Two weeks after our poor performance at Harlow, we had a very good opportunity of putting things right on some excellent hawking land in rural Bedfordshire. Since Harlow Ami had made a few more kills, one, I am proud to say, a 3.2 kg (7 lb) hare in Hertfordshire. Whatever had upset her, and I still did not know what it was for sure, it seemed she was back to her usual obedient self.

At the meet were two other Harris hawks, a male and a female, a male redtail and a Finnish female goshawk, which I was itching to see fly. The quarry was mainly rabbit but there were, we were told, the odd pheasant or two scattered around.

We began the day by forming a line and beating some woodland. A rabbit bolted and the female Harris hawk was slipped in hot pursuit, weaving in between the low branches, flying fast and precise. The rabbit ran towards a large fallen tree trunk, hesitated and was caught. The goshawk had second slip but Roger had asked if he could miss his turn in favour of slipping should a pheasant get up. We ventured further into the woodland, still holding the line, still beating the thick covert. A second rabbit bolted and began its run to safety. This time it was the little male Harris hawk that gave chase. Flying at a mere 595 g (1 lb 5oz), he was like lightning, small and light, but an experienced and proficient hunter. There was no way the rabbit was going to escape, and it was caught in fine style. Next it was the turn of Bob's three-year-old male redtail which always gave a good account of himself. He was a massive bird who would attempt to kill anything. Bob likes to fly via trees and as it was his slip, all other birds were held firmly on the fist. Jim, our beater, had spotted an inviting warren and a little jill ferret was placed inside. The redtail was now directly above, watching the warren from a branch; he knew exactly what was going on. Something higher up caught his eye, however, and he was off. It was a grey squirrel. Bob neither likes nor encourages his male to fly squirrel but this is a hazard of hawking in this terrain. The redtail was cork-screwing the tree, trying to grab the squirrel without getting bitten himself. This style of hawking is tremendously exciting, full of action. Bob stood below with a rat on the glove, desperately trying to get his bird back under control, but it was the best part of thirty minutes before the hawk gave up and returned to the fist. Although he had not made a kill, he did give us some top-quality action.

Next it was Ami's turn. We had almost reached the end of the woodland and decided to make our way along some covert that was approximately 50 m wide. Gypsy was given his head and Ami started to get fired up. All the other birds stood off whilst the dog worked. A rabbit bolted, Gypsy stood still and Ami gave chase, twisting and turning. She thrust out a foot and missed, landing temporarily on the ground but maintained her momentum and continued the pursuit. Again she caught up with the rabbit but again she just missed. The rabbit ran into cover and Ami was left without a kill. It was, however, a spectacular flight which the rabbit was extremely fortunate to escape.

It was a further hour or so before Ami had a second chance. In between, the goshawk took a rabbit at lightning speed, although it was not the hardest of slips, and Bob's redtail also got a kill. Towards the end of the day Ami was finally rewarded, again in woodland. Gypsy marked and flushed a rabbit and Ami was instantly in pursuit. The rabbit appeared to enter some cover, so Ami pulled off and took vantage in a tree. I was some way away with a restricted view, but Bob was in a good position. I could see Ami on the branch, and I saw her jolt forward from time to time, as if about to leave, but she kept hesitating. It was obvious that the rabbit was still about, as she was fully focused on a spot below her. I ran towards her and saw her leave the branch, disappearing behind some bramble. She was now out of sight, but the squeal of the rabbit told me she had made contact. According to Bob, the rabbit left the bramble, hopped onto a thick tree trunk and as it leaped towards the ground Ami grabbed it in mid-air.

That day in Bedfordshire was for me the best meet to date. Every bird flew well and all were rewarded with kills. Bob's redtail made two kills, as did the goshawk – although not on pheasant or duck as Roger had hoped.

Field meeting – Llandrindod Wells

Llandrindod Wells was to be our last large field meet of the season. I received an invitation from a friend in Abergavenny who was putting together five birds for an 800 ha (2000 acre) plot in a beautiful part of Wales. Quarry was mainly rabbit and I was allowed a guest. I had been to

Llandrindnod Wells many years before for a holiday and clearly remembered its outstanding countryside. Because of the distance, Bob and I drove up the previous evening and stayed in a friend's cottage approximately 25 miles from the venue.

On this meet were a golden eagle, a female goshawk, a female Harris hawk flying at 1162 g (2lb 9oz), Bob's male redtail and Ami. It was going to be a good day for me, as my name was drawn from the hat first. The dog on this outing was the beater's liver and white English springer spaniel, a breed Ami had not flown over before.

It was decided that we should work what seemed an endless sea of semi-rough covert with blades of grass just long enough to hide a rabbit. We held a line and began to beat, and a rabbit bolted between myself and Bob, who was approximately 3 m (10 ft) to my right, and headed my way. Ami left the fist, and in the blink of an eye had made the simplest of kills. This had been far too easy, a gift as they say, so I went in, dispatched the rabbit and placed it in the bag. Rabbits were bolting everywhere, in all directions, sending all the unhooded birds into bating attacks.

By the time we had worked this area, all the birds except the eagle had killed. By lunch-time Ami had killed twice, the second resulting from a longer, more challenging slip, again on rabbit. I allowed her the rare privilege of using the trees whilst the dog worked below her. When a rabbit did bolt she flew it with the authority which I have come to expect from her, twisting and turning, using her head to determine her prey's next move. She deserved this kill, she had flown it well and obviously saw the dog as a companion and not a threat. In normal circumstances I would have rewarded her heavily, but it was only barely lunchtime and we still had a further afternoon's hawking to get through.

After a good meal in the local pub and a pint of their finest to keep the chill out, it was back to the field. Ami had made the last kill before our break, so it was quite some time before she was in action again. Unfortunately the golden eagle retired after lunch, which was disappointing as it would have been nice to see him in action. Moving on, we proceeded by working a large carp lake which was known for its duck, moorhen and coot. The springer worked like crazy but other than a single flight for the goshawk on a scampering moorhen, there was nothing. Back in the woodland, the female Harris was slipped onto a squirrel. She was a seasoned hawk who was apparently dynamite on this quarry. She worked the tree, showing her fitness. The squirrel, also fit and agile, sprang from tree top to tree top, racing around in a frenzied bid to outwit the hawk, but no matter how hard it tried the Harris was there, with it all the way. Finally the bird grabbed her target and was allowed to feed up as it was getting late in the day.

After a further kill for Bob's redtail on an unsuspecting rabbit and a further flight resulting in an unlucky escape for Ami's target, we called it a day. It had been a long way for Bob, me and our birds to travel, but it was a day which we shall both treasure and I thank all those concerned for a privileged invitation.

With Ami's first season coming to an end, I only had one final goal, to get her entered on squirrel.

Alternative hawking methods

Many of today's falconers, especially, it seems, those who are restricted to weekend flying, attempt to flush quarry by thrashing a beating stick against cover. Rarely will they try other methods, which can be a major mistake. I have known falconers to beat cover in exactly this way for well over twenty years. It is of course a tried and tested method of providing quarry for one's hawk, but it is a pity to limit yourself to this, as you could be missing out on other aspects of hawking which you really would enjoy.

The use of dogs and ferrets can make a great a difference to a day's hunting, often producing quarry when it would otherwise have been scarce. I remember walking a dense hedgerow one season with a male goshawk. I beat the entire length and was rather surprised not to produce anything for my bird. A friend of mine walked the very same hedge, approximately fifteen minutes later, working his dog, and produced rabbit after rabbit. A working partner of this calibre is worth a great deal to one's sport.

Although walking through picturesque countryside, armed with a bird of prey in search of quarry, could never be regarded as boring, I would regard it as somewhat monotonous, as there is so much variety for one to explore. Falconry is not only about the size of the bag at the end of day or season, it is also about enjoying what nature and the countryside have to offer; this is why it is so appealing and addictive. Day after day throughout the hawking season I walk the very same hedgerows. I am fully aware of every single rabbit warren, every blade of grass, but never in all these years have I been bored, as there is always something new to see.

In addition to beating cover with a stick, falconry can offer other forms of hunting which can bring further excitement. One can fly from horseback or off-road vehicles or at night.

The number of horse riders I have passed on a Sunday morning, whilst walking along a country lane with my bird on my arm must run into many hundreds. In a roundabout sort of way we are not too dissimilar, as we both have a love and dedication for our animals and for the countryside where we pursue our sport. Usually such meetings result in a quick acknowledgement of one another before we continue on our separate ways, but occasionally a friendship has blossomed and I have ended up teaching them falconry in return for some valuable riding time. Next to raptors, horses are my second passion. I love their character, their intelligence and the intimate bond between them and their owners. To this day

I still enjoy a Boxing Day cross-country hack and I make good use of the long moulting months to ride out every week. Unfortunately, owning such a beast would be a massive commitment which I could not aspire to. Eagle-Owl Falconry keeps me far too busy, and eats up too much of my money to allow me a further passion.

Although I have ridden from an early age I could not be described quite as a Harvey Smith or Nick Skelton, but, I am reasonably confident on horseback and feel safe when aboard, which is all that one needs to enjoy a wonderful day. Another benefit of this exchange is that one does not have to find the time to tend to the animal which, believe me, is as hard as tending to any bird. Rarely will one be in the privileged position of owning both a bird and a horse, so a proposition like this is an excellent alternative and one you should look out for if you are at all interested.

And hunting from horseback is well worth trying if ever the chance occurs. It permits one to cover much more ground, giving more scope. Here at Eagle-Owl Falconry, it is our intention to put together hunting days solely from horseback for those who have some riding experience. There are, however, one or two golden rules for those who would like to go on to hawk in this way.

Your bird must obviously be made to the horse and vice versa. I have seen both birds and horses react extremely violently when brought into close proximity. It is not difficult, however, and it is often far easier to make a Harris to a horse than to a dog. I have used and seen many Harrises flown via horseback and I have never had any serious behavioural problems or vices to contend with. Once the bird understands that this big beast means her no harm you will be in the position to enjoy falconry to the very full, as did our royalty many years ago.

It is wise, and at our falconry school it will be a requirement, to have relevant riding experience. You will not enjoy this style of hawking if you do not feel comfortable sitting on horseback, as you will only have one hand for the reins and your backside will not be able to take too much pounding from the rise and fall of the horses motion. Moreover, there is always the risk of being thrown and sustaining a severe injury. So take a course of lessons from one of the hundreds of schools operating around the country.

With those provisos, a competent bird, a steady horse and a dog working in close harmony is, in my opinion, falconry at its very finest.

Another method which can be full of fun and excitement is to go off road in a suitable four-wheel-drive vehicle. Here organisation and driving ability are of paramount importance; on more than one occasion have I seen vehicles stuck in muddy bogs or on their side due to the driver exceeding its capabilities. Although I occasionally go hawking this way it has to be said that I am not overly enthusiastic. If we are in pursuit of rabbits, I believe the vehicle can spook them long before we have even spotted them running for cover. I was brought up to be as quiet as possible

28) *Hawking from a four-wheel drive vehicle*

when searching for quarry. Rabbits have excellent hearing and are hard enough to surprise at the best of times, so for me this method of hawking is best left to others.

If this method of hunting appeals to you, you must be careful not to break the law, which is full of complications regarding hawking quarry from a motorised vehicle, unknowingly. It is advisable therefore to check the latest legislation and become fully conversant with its many delicate areas. Harris hawks will take comfortably to this style of hawking, but as with anything that can cause upset and panic, the bird must be allowed to get used to the vehicle and the vast undulating terrain over which you will be tracking.

Another form of hawking is flying at night. I have done very little of this but I have friends and colleagues who enjoy it so much that come a starry and windy night they can be seen heading straight for the open fields.

A strong beam of light is used to find the quarry. When a rabbit is caught in this beam, the hawk is released from the fist in pursuit. As a bird of prey can see no better than ourselves at night, it is important that the beam is on the rabbit at all times or the bird has no chance of a kill and may even do herself an injury by crashing into a fence or other obstacles. Land which has been heavily lamped upon, as this form of hunting is called, may result in the rabbits becoming lamp-shy, meaning they will bolt straight for cover as soon as the beam is visible. To overcome this,

(29) Lamping

falconers use a coloured filter over the white beam in a bid to outwit their target and keep it sitting still in the open for as long as possible.

Organisation is the key to successful night hawking and the bird must be trained accordingly or you risk losing her. It is also wise to use telemetry. Friends of mine have hawks which are used solely for night flying; their manning and training was carried out at night, and this is all they know. Harris hawks will take quite easily to this style of hawking, and can excel at it. Hunting in this way is also a great alternative for those who have little time during the day, as a bird, if it is well trained, will hunt as proficiently at night as it will during the day.

Whether on foot, on horseback, from a jeep, during the day or at night, falconry has its ups and downs and risks, which will be different in each style. Try out its various forms and enjoy what each one has to offer. Although I greatly enjoy riding, flying from horseback will take me many more years to perfect, just like the team work which goes into successful night flying.

IMPORTANT INFORMATION

Breeding Harris hawks

by Paul Harris

Over the years raptor breeders have done so much to stabilise and reintroduce many endangered species back into the wild. Certain owls, for instance, might now be extinct if it were not for the drive and determination of such people. The barn owl (*Tyto alba*) instantly springs to mind. This little bird has suffered more than any other from loss of habitat and poisoning. Although breeding barn owls in captivity is simplicity itself, it is an extremely difficult task to release them into the wild with measurable success. Various groups and individuals attempted it but many birds were found dead or dying due to the unsuitability of the chosen release sites. These releases were no doubt carried out in good faith but solid groundwork and an in-depth knowledge of the barn owl's biology and natural needs are required if one is to stand any chance of success.

As a consequence of these devastating, unregulated release schemes, the Government put a halt to them, and it is now illegal to release barn owls unless a licence is firstly obtained from the Department of the Environment, Transport and the Regions. Some individuals and groups did have success, however, as their dedication to locating and examining potential release sites was followed up by thorough investigative work to ensure that all went smoothly once the owls were released. This helped tremendously to give the barn owl's wild population some stability. With further conservation work from organisations such as Raptor Rescue, which rehabilitates and reintroduces injured birds of prey back into the wild, the outlook for our more susceptible indigenous raptors and owls is now optimistic. Other raptors, such as red kites and peregrine falcons have been victims of man's own selfishness and petty greed, and as a consequence are highly protected.

In the UK, it has long been illegal to take birds of prey from the wild for the purposes of falconry, and those who do so face imprisonment or heavy fines. Therefore, the potential owner has to locate and purchase a captive-bred eyass from one of the many reputable breeders scattered around the country. Unfortunately, it has to be said that not all breeders – a more apt description would be dealers – are trustworthy, honourable and caring of their birds, and you are well advised to steer clear of such people. To this day, illegal birds are being exchanged and sold, as are those which have not been acceptably reared. The beginner especially, should only purchase an eyass of the year from someone who has been recommended to him. Never be fooled into buying hawks which are ridiculously cheap, and always ask for certain health guarantees. Be on your guard, and if you are purchasing from a magazine advertisement, be sure to take someone with you who has a good general knowledge of birds of prey. Retain the seller's name, address and phone number and keep all correspondence in a safe place.

The modern falconer has an unprecedented choice when it comes to obtaining birds of prey. Through successful breeding programmes, raptors and owls have never been in such abundance and little thought needs to be given to a species' availability as it once was. Although this is good for the dedicated falconer, it can also put ideas into the heads of those who only have one thing on their mind, namely money. Whilst it is true that breeders can make a good income from producing certain raptors, if one relied on Harris hawks, one would most certainly starve. The price for birds such as these is at an all-time low, even though demand is still high. This is due to the ease with which they are bred and the number of new breeders we see each season. So competition to sell youngsters is fierce, and price reductions are available like never before. I for one would not have envisaged that Harris hawks would be as cheap as they are today. These low prices will, I am sure, never apply to other birds, such as merlins, goshawks or peregrines, birds which bring the breeder better financial rewards but demand a much more intensive knowledge and touch. Artificial insemination is now widely practised, as the demand for hybrid falcons grows steadily each year. Even semen from a tiercel is being sold and can be posted directly to your door. Captive breeding really has come on in leaps and bounds, and birds which breeders are having difficulties in producing today will, no doubt, tomorrow be easily purchased, and have a competitive price tag to match.

Those who are thinking of breeding birds of prey, either part time as a hobby or with the view to earning a living, should make no mistake about the time and initial investment which will be incurred. A great deal of thought should be given to the many aspects involved, as you are entering into a world full of heartache, and potentially wasted years, living on false hopes, maybes and 'if onlys'. No one can put two birds together and know for sure that they will produce offspring. One has to be patient and give the birds time, and this can involve years of waiting with still no youngsters to show off. If you want to breed birds of prey then it is important that you do so for the might reasons, as the financial returns can be a very long time coming, if at all. The modern falconer requires top-quality hawks at modest prices.

A typical breeding season for me begins around late February to early March. As the hunting season draws to an end and my goshawk is put down for her moult, instead of looking forward to a few months' rest, my male Harris hawk starts making low-pitched groaning sounds. He then begins to take food up to the female by the nest side. The nest I have made for my birds is a car tyre that is placed upon a high level platform containing peat and river-washed sand. The tyre is filled with this mixture, which retains humidity and protects the eggs. Some 20 mm gravel is packed upon the platform to a height of 2.5 cm (1 in). From this moment on my workload intensifies as each day passes by.

It is my strong belief that once a pair has bonded this bond should not be broken, as it may lead to greater success eventually. Birds need to establish themselves to one another and this, I believe, is best done by leaving a pair together all year. Harris hawks bond for life. In the wild they stay together season after season. They do not come together purely for the purposes of breeding, and you are well advised to remember this. Those who put two birds together just for the breeding season may indeed achieve a result, but these birds will never bond as heavily as those which are together always and this could result in small clutch sizes and mortality.

It is important that before the male naturally commences his display to the female, the breeder should enter the aviary and clip back both hawks' talons and spray for mites. The aviary should be thoroughly cleaned, preferably with a solution of Vircon S, as it will be some time before the breeder can enter it again.

Feeding twice a day begins around early March, and by late March the first egg will be laid. Further eggs will be produced at two-day intervals, although they will not necessarily hatch at two-day intervals. Incubation is between twenty-nine and thirty-one days, and begins when the final egg is laid.

Diet is extremely important. It is vital that quality foods are fed before the courtship begins, while it is going on and when the babies pip and begin rapidly growing. Good food containing a mixture of nutritional values will give the youngsters the healthy start that they so desperately need, and will help develop their fragile bones.

It is vital that the breeder constantly monitors the progress of the babies and the health of the laying mother, especially if she is inexperienced. If she is not sitting or shows signs that she will break the eggs then they will need to be removed and placed either beneath a foster parent or in an incubator. It is the breeder's responsibility to see that all runs smoothly, identifying potential problems and getting them sorted out quickly and in a professional way. This intense monitoring can be very time-consuming and trying, but it is an essential part of the breeding process. It takes much

much more to produce healthy young than just placing two birds of the opposite sex together, keeping one's fingers crossed and hoping.

Providing that all goes smoothly, the babies are left with the parents for approximately twelve weeks and can then be sold as parent-reared birds. Parent-reared Harris hawks will be less likely to scream and mantle over a kill and should not be nasty or aggressive towards the falconer, which reduces the potential for bloody accidents in the field. Only in special circumstances, and to experienced falconers, will I supply younger hawks for imprinting. There really is little to be gained from purchasing an imprinted Harris hawk and the disadvantages will, without doubt, far outweigh any advantages. The only time my young see a human is when I go into the aviary to slip on the identity ring, which I do quickly and with minimal fuss. Unless a bird has somehow injured itself, they have no further human contact until they are caught up for the purchaser.

It has always been my policy to be as open as I possibly can with my clients, although one must constantly be careful with new enquiries, as not every purchaser is honourable. It could be that they are using conversations and early meetings to 'case' my premises, my security measures and my livestock. I can understand therefore why some breeders prefer to keep a low profile; who could blame them when bird theft is at its present level. It does not mean that they have anything to hide; it is a case of protecting one's stock as best one can.

When I receive an enquiry, I invite the potential purchaser round to my premises for an informal chat. They are welcome to look around and ask questions. They are shown the aviaries where their bird is to be reared, and the breeding stock. I give them an idea of the way the season should go and will only take a deposit if I feel they have the ability to look after the hawk correctly. Most experienced falconers and breeders can tell if someone is bluffing, and knows far less than they pretend. Beginners are welcome to purchase from me but I need to be confident that they have the grounding to look after a bird which I have worked so hard to produce.

I can supply references from previous purchasers if clients wish, and should everything go well at this meeting, and I feel the person has the basic ability to justify owning a bird, then I will take a holding deposit and keep them fully informed throughout the breeding season as to the progress of their bird. They are welcome to make a return visit to check on their bird themselves should they wish.

It is always my intention to supply Harris hawks which are in tip-top condition, healthy and strong. The hours I put in throughout the season, I hope, helps me to achieve this. It is not a case of money, as many believe; there is very little money in breeding Harrises. The pleasure is in producing and logging the progress of the birds when they go to their new homes. I always ask the purchaser to keep me informed of the hawk's progress throughout the season, how the training went and the bird's

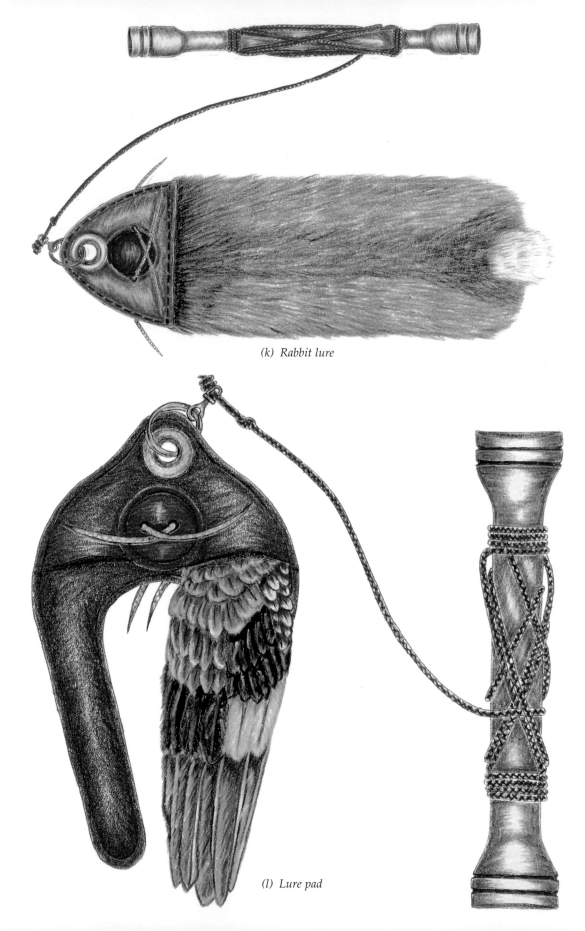

(k) Rabbit lure

(l) Lure pad

(m) Ami suspended in mid-air

(n) Ami sitting on the balance scales

aptitude in the field. It is this which gives me more pleasure than money could ever do.

For those who do have an interest in breeding Harris hawks I would urge you to give the matter intense thought. First, as many breeders will tell you, it is far easier and safer to fly birds of prey than pair two off and hope they will produce young. Captive breeding requires planning, dedication, knowledge, effort and investment, and even then there are no guarantees. Falconers are not stupid, they know what they want and how the end result should be. Immaculate rearing and a solid diet are therefore vital, and will contribute ten-fold to the bird's eventual good health and performance in the field.

As with breeding dogs, it is important to know why you are doing it. Can you find homes for the young? Can you find the time to monitor the youngsters' progress? Have you the funds to begin, and how many years can you go without receiving any return? Do you have the knowledge? Just as it is important that beginners to falconry attend a course, so it is for those who want to breed. One will learn so much more than from just reading books and watching videos. Most successful breeders keep their techniques and knowledge to themselves, so it is very difficult to get solid information. Think about the birds which make breeding financially viable and how you can reach the market. Again, a course that is dedicated to breeding birds of prey will answer your questions, including some which you have not yet even thought about.

Harris hawks are very common throughout the UK and 90 per cent of my enquiries each season are from those wanting this species. Although they are not difficult to breed in comparison to other raptors, the breeder will need to be available during the season to check that the mother bird remains healthy and undistressed during laying and that the babies do not encounter life-threatening problems during pipping. Some breeders, although I use this term loosely, have been known to leave their birds to their own devices during this period, then later discover that the mother has broken the eggs or is not sitting. The end result is no youngsters. My life revolves around the birds, and at this time of year nothing else is more important.

For all my time and hard work, the financial returns are very modest. Producing quality Harris hawks is becoming less viable each season. I sometimes think I am only breeding because the parents are a bonded pair which have served me well over many years. Should anything happen to either bird, then I would be extremely reluctant to find a replacement.

During my breeding career there have been many ups and downs, many happy moments and many sad. Remember, breeding hawks must be done for the right reasons. Money ought to be irrelevant; gone are the days when there were too few birds for too many purchasers.

Health checks
by Philip Stapelberg, BVSc (Pret), MRCVS

As far as raptors are concerned, Harris hawks are probably one of the hardiest species kept in captivity. This makes them ideally suited to beginners. Although they may be easier to take care of, a high standard of husbandry, nutrition and health monitoring is still necessary to ensure continued good health. In this section I will discuss some of the health issues that may affect your bird, how to recognise disease and most importantly, how to prevent it.

Parasites
There are a number of different parasites that can be found living on, or inside the bodies of raptors. They can be divided into:

- ectoparasites
- endoparasites
- haemoparasites (blood parasites)

Ectoparasites usually occur on the feathers or skin and include organisms such as ticks, mites, lice and biting flies. Most ectoparasites do not cause any typical symptoms unless the particular bird's immune system is depressed. A notable exception is a heavy biting lice *(Mallophaga)* infestation. This could lead to severe itching, irritability and self-inflicted trauma. Usually a topical ectoparasite powder can be used to get rid of the mites. Ivermectin can also be used. This drug can be administered orally or by injection, and will usually be repeated within ten to fourteen days. Treating birds, whether it is for parasites or any other disease, must always be done under the guidance of a veterinarian and should never be attempted by unqualified people, including the falconer himself.

Another frequently encountered ectoparasite is the hippoboscid fly which belongs to the genus *Pseudolynchia*. This is a flattened winged insect that can usually be seen as it scurries for cover under the feathers whilst one is examining them and the skin. *Pseudolynchia* flies feed on the blood of their host, which is sucked through modified mouthparts from the superficial blood vessels just underneath the bird's skin. They are considered to be involved in the transmission of blood-borne parasites. Even though these flies are normally not associated with clinical signs they can contribute to disease, especially in weakened individuals.

Endoparasites is the collective name used to describe internal parasites such as nematodes, trematodes and cestodes. These groups are known to most people as roundworms, flatworms and tapeworms. Worms are not the only internal parasite of importance. Protozoans, especially *Trichomonas* spp., are common disease-causing parasites in birds of prey. These endoparasites most commonly affect the gastrointestinal system.

Worm infestations can go undetected, but if the parasite load is very high it may cause symptoms such as regurgitation, loss of appetite, weight loss, diarrhoea, depression and head-flicking. It is important to have birds checked at least once a year for parasites. A number of simple tests, such as faecal flotations, faecal wet preparations, faecal smears, crop smears, crop content wet preparations, examination of cast material etc., can be done by your veterinarian to check your bird for internal parasites. Once the parasite involved has been identified, your vet can treat the bird for that specific parasite. There is no such thing as an all-round dewormer. Treatment differs for different parasites and is only ever effective when treated specifically, with the correct drug at the correct dosage.

Trichomonas causes a condition known as frounce, characterised by raised white, cheesy lesions in the mouth, pharynx and crop. This protozoan endoparasite also occurs in wild pigeons. Raptors are infected when they eat infected prey animals such as pigeons and gamebirds. Frounce is treatable, usually with metronidazole. A diagnosis is usually made by examining crop wet preparations and crop smears under the microscope. There are other conditions that resemble frounce, which again underlines the importance of a specific veterinary diagnosis. Diseases that cause similar symptoms are:

- candidiasis, a single-celled fungal infection
- capillariasis, a type of worm infestation
- bacterial abscesses
- some herpes and pox-virus infections
- Hypovitaminosis A

Blood parasites are usually protozoan parasites that live inside the blood stream. They are less important than the others and only rarely affect captive-bred birds of prey. The most important blood parasites are *Plasmodium* spp., so-called avian malaria. It is good if raptor owners are at least aware of the existence of blood parasites, but detailed discussion of the subject is beyond the scope of this section.

Feather-plucking

Feather-plucking refers to the condition where birds pull out their own feathers. It is a very common problem in psittacines (parrots), but relatively uncommon in raptors, with the exception of the Harris hawk. Harris hawks are the only psychotic feather-pluckers amongst raptorial birds. Psychotic refers to psychological disturbances which lead to a change in personality and behaviour that is not normal. Birds used for public displays and birds kept in weatherings with limited views, such as those with four solid sides with only an open-meshed roof, are more likely to feather-pluck. Harris hawks are very intelligent birds compared to other raptors and can therefore get bored very easily if stimulation is lacking. They usually pluck the undersides of their breasts and their inner thighs clean. Once the psychotic behaviour has been going for a while it may become habitual and such a vice can be difficult to stop. Special emphasis should be placed on mental stimulation, in order to prevent boredom and the resultant feather-plucking. Weatherings should have at least one open-meshed wall to enable the bird to see beyond the confines of her enclosure. Toys such as tennis balls may also help to prevent this condition.

Treatment can be problematic if it is not started early. Darkness or hooding should be the first step. A change of scenery may also help. Certain behaviour-modifying drugs have been used with success but they should be a last resort. Consult your veterinarian as soon as unusual feather loss or plucking is noted.

Fungal diseases

Aspergillosis is a fungal disease which primarily affects the respiratory tract of birds (the windpipe bronchi, airsacs and lungs). Although the fungus can cause other types of infections, most problems are caused when susceptible birds inhale its spores. These settle, usually in the airsacs, and this leads to fungal growth inside the bird's body. The inflammatory process that occurs as a result of this growth leads to the formation of granulomas (accumulations of fungal hyphae, which is the term used to describe the filament or branch-like structure of certain fungi, and inflammatory material). It is usually only when these granulomas start to interfere with the normal respiratory function that symptoms appear and veterinary help is called in. Unfortunately this may already be too late to treat this condition successfully.

For this reason, the emphasis should be on prevention and not on treatment. The most important principles of disease prevention in general are:

- Prevent exposure to the disease-causing agent (in this case fungal spores).
- Maintain a healthy, functional immune system.
- Use prophylactic medication correctly where indicated.
- Vaccinate against disease where possible.

There is at present, no vaccine available against this disease so you will need to use the other measures suggested.

Aspergillus fumigatus is a ubiquitous saprophyte that grows on almost any organic matter. The fungus prefers moist, dark areas with limited ventilation. Birds should therefore be kept in dry, well-lit areas with good ventilation. Your weathering should be well away from rotting organic material such as wood piles and compost heaps. The area where you keep your bird must also be kept clean. Faeces and absorbent materials must be cleaned out regularly and not allowed to build up. The biggest source of infection is mouldy travel boxes. When birds are confined in such a small space filled with millions of fungal spores, they are very likely to get aspergillosis. Travel boxes should be kept impeccably clean, and never stored where they are likely to get wet or damp. Leave them open in a well-lit room rather than in the back of a dark and dirty shed or other out-building. If you are aware of the risks, you should be able to limit the possibility of exposure to the minimum.

Your bird's immune system can be enhanced by sound husbandry and proper nutrition to start with. A good mineral and vitamin supplement should be added to the diet and certain homeopathic remedies such as Echinacea may enhance your bird's immune system. Speak to your veterinary surgeon and other experienced falconers about husbandry and nutrition. A very important principle in maintaining a healthy immune system is to avoid conditions that could suppress its function. A good example is stress. Continued stress will decrease any bird's ability to fight disease. Although a certain amount of stress is unavoidable, it must be prevented wherever possible. Respiratory stressors such as cigarette smoke, dusty environments and aerosol sprays near birds should also be avoided. The airway's defence systems are weakened by these stressors and this will enable pathogens such as fungal spores to enter with ease.

Fortunately Harris hawks are not regarded as a high risk species when it comes to aspergillosis, so the use of prophylactic medicine is not usually required. However, it is still a very serious problem that all owners of birds of prey should be aware of.

The symptoms of aspergillosis can be very vague in the early stages. It may suddenly get worse after a period of stress. Usually birds start to lose weight, with or without a good appetite, and may become depressed. Regurgitation or vomiting may be observed and breathing difficulties usually develop as the disease worsens. Diagnosis can be very challenging in the early stages, and it usually requires blood tests, radiographs, cultures, endoscopy and histopathology to confirm the diagnosis. If diagnosed early the condition may be cured with intensive antifungal treatment in hospital but the prognosis in most cases is usually poor. Many birds lose their lives to this condition and some are humanely destroyed to prevent further suffering. It can be referred to as the silent killer, but adopting the principles discussed here will lower the risk of your bird contracting this awful disease.

Candidiasis is another fungal condition caused by *Candida albicans*, a single-celled fungus that grows opportunistically, usually in the gastrointestinal system. It is mainly a secondary pathogen found in immuno-suppressed individuals or birds with other underlying health problems. This means that healthy, well-kept birds usually do not suffer from it. Treatment with antibiotics could also be responsible for candidal growth because of the effect it has on the normal intestinal flora of the gastrointestinal tract. When normal competitive micro-organisms are diminished, as is the case with antibiotic treatment, candida may flourish. It is for this reason that birds must be monitored for its occurrence whilst being treated with antibiotics.

Candidiasis can be treated with Nystatin, although some strains may exhibit resistance to this drug and alternative antifungal treatments should then be used. The condition is usually diagnosed when crop or faecal smears are examined under the microscope.

Bacterial diseases

The most important bacterial condition is bumblefoot. This is a common and very serious condition that affects the weight-bearing surfaces of the feet. Harris hawks are less susceptible to bumblefoot than other species such as longwings, but any raptor is at risk, especially if proper preventative care is not taken. Owners should also be able to recognise this condition. The earlier it is seen to by a qualified veterinarian the better the chances of successful treatment.

The symptoms of bumblefoot depend on the severity or the stage of the condition. In the early stages there may only be a thinning of the skin, with the area being warm to the touch. Eventually the dermal papillae, which are raised bumps on the underside of the toes, will become smooth and the surrounding skin may show signs of inflammation. The next step, as the condition gets worse, is for the superficial layers of the skin to become detached from the deeper layers. It is now easy for bacteria to enter the area. The result is an active infection that will progressively worsen. The bacterial infection can result in damage to flexor tendons, bones and joints. Pain, crusts and wounds draining fluid or pus may be noticed in these cases. Bumblefoot can also be complicated by the entry of fungi into the wound. Candida is often isolated from these infected areas.

The causes of bumblefoot are varied but usually abnormally sustained pressure on the soles of the feet eventually leads to its development. This pressure results from:

- birds being overweight or obese, or not flown enough and allowed to become fat and lazy
- hard, unyielding perches that are not fitted with adequate padding such as astroturf
- an injury to one limb which leads to sustained weight-bearing on the other so that that foot carries the whole body weight.

Other causes include repeated, uncontrolled bating which may damage the feet, although unlike sparrowhawks and goshawks, Harris hawks are not highly strung birds, and are less likely to bate excessively. Wounds caused by bites from prey animals such as squirrels and puncture wounds from talons are also possible causes. Finally, bumblefoot could also occur in diseased or debilitated birds that are suffering from other medical conditions.

Once bumblefoot has been diagnosed it should be treated promptly and aggressively. During the early stages, treatment involves correcting possible underlying problems such as obesity and treating with antibiotics. Antibiotic treatment must always be based on the results of a bacterial culture sensitivity test. This test enables vets to choose the best antibiotic for the job. Disinfecting perches and wounds topically is also important. Povidone iodine or chlorhexidine is usually used. If the condition is more severe it may be necessary to drain and clean out infected areas surgically. Hydroactive dressings and protective dressings such as ball-bandages are often required. Surgery may have to be repeated more than once to cure severe cases. Neglected or long-standing cases can be notoriously difficult to cure and may require the bird to be put down. It is one of those health issues that must always be taken seriously.

Nutritional conditions of young birds

There are a few developmental conditions that are directly related to nutrition of young birds. For this reason I strongly advise owners to take newly purchased birds for a veterinary check up. The growth and development of the young Harris hawk and its skeletal system is dependent on proper nutrition.

Calcium is important to development. Meat without bone contains almost no calcium and it is also high in phosphate which disrupts the calcium/phosphate ratio inside the bird's body, which can lead to various skeletal abnormalities. The condition is known as nutritional osteodystrophy and results in weak birds with poorly calcified bones that break easily. The condition can be complicated by other dietary deficiencies but the feeding of carcasses containing small digestible bone rather than only meat lowers the incidence of osteodystrophy. Full-body radiographs should be taken to assess the skeletal health of these birds. Harris hawks which are bred in captivity should only be purchased from reputable breeders who feed a correct balanced diet.

Recognising disease

This is only an introduction to some of the more important health issues you may encounter. It is not intended to be comprehensive but rather selectively informative, so that inexperienced falconers and beginners can be aware of important health issues. My hope is that it will stimulate interest and encourage further reading.

In order to recognise disease, one must first be able to recognise health. The best way to do this is to follow a five-point monitoring plan, which will enable you to detect any deviations from the norm. The plan is as follows:

- Monitor your bird's food intake on a daily basis. The best way to do this is to weigh the portions being fed. Note feeding behaviour so that any change in appetite or behaviour can be addressed.
- Monitor your bird's weight. This is usually done in accordance with food intake. Weigh her daily, and if any weight is lost despite the bird having a good appetite, it could mean that there is something wrong. This will also help to prevent your bird from becoming overweight.
- Monitor stools and casts for frequency, appearance and smell. Note the texture, the amount of fluid present or any abnormalities such as loose stools.
- Observe your bird's behaviour for at least twenty minutes every day. Pay attention to breathing, alertness and activities such as preening. It is preferable that this is done whilst the bird is at rest and not stressed.
- Take your bird for veterinary check-up once a year. Have a faecal sample and cast sample examined for parasites, and have a complete blood count done. This will provide your veterinarian with important information on your bird's health.

Follow this five-point plan and have any deviation or change from that which is normal checked should it last for more than forty-eight hours. It is far easier and cheaper to treat disease early. Prevention is always better than cure and it is pointless to wait until a bird is really sick before taking it to the vet. Raptors are very delicate animals and neglecting health issues will often lead to suffering and death.

First aid

Accidents may occur whilst you are out hunting or at a time when the services of a vet are not immediately available. It is therefore important to carry a basic first-aid kit with you at all times. I advise that it should contain at least the following items, which must always be kept clean and disinfected:

- a syringe and feeding tube which can be used to administer fluids and electrolytes to birds in shock; your veterinarian should be able to demonstrate the technique for this
- a small blanket, towel or space blanket to restrain your bird or prevent hypothermia
- a pair of tweezers to remove foreign bodies or dirt from wounds before disinfecting
- disinfecting solution such as povidone iodine or chlorhexidine, also swabs, cotton-tip applicators and cotton wool
- bandaging materials such as Vetrap and micropore to immobilise damaged limbs or to dress wounds
- a flexible finger splint to splint fractured bones
- some 4/0 sterile catgut and haemostat to stop life-threatening haemorrhage

- an electrolyte solution such as Ringers Lactate or Hartmans solution to administer via a crop tube if necessary
- a silver nitrate pencil to stop bleeding from a damaged talon or beak tip
- your veterinarian's business card or telephone number and a mobile phone

Your veterinarian can give you a short course on how to use these first-aid accessories. This is important to enable you to have the skill and confidence to apply first aid in the field.

When applying first aid, the important principles are:

- Stop any bleeding and treat for shock.
- Provide heat.
- Immobilise fractures to prevent further damage and pain.
- Clean and disinfect wounds.
- Seek veterinary help as soon as possible.

In conclusion it is fair to summarise the Harris hawk as hardy, very intelligent and very special. If we take care of them properly, they should provide us with hours of enjoyment.

The annual moult

When I was a young lad, all enthusiastic and learning about falconry, I was quite upset when I was told that the hunting season consisted of only six months out of the twelve. The reasons for this were the open season for legally taking quarry and the annual moult. These days, after a long, hectic season battling against the cold, wind and rain, I tend to welcome this period as a time to recharge the fading batteries. It is also a good time to evaluate the condition of one's weatherings, equipment etc.

Although the Harris hawk, could be flown continuously throughout the year, it is common practice for austringers to allow their hawks a resting period. During this time, the bird is fed full rations, rarely handled and never flown, but given the opportunity of dropping old feathers in place for newer, healthier ones.

Throughout a hawk's life there are many plumage changes. An eyass of the year is born with a short, fluffy covering known as down. This is replaced by a second, thicker down after a couple of weeks which, to a degree, allows the youngster to control its own body temperature. Once the hawk reaches full body weight, the juvenile plumage appears. The hawk stays in this plumage until the major moult, which occurs during the first spring of hatching, and by the autumn she is in full adult plumage.

In the UK, the hawking season is active from September or October, depending on the birds being flown and the height of cover, through to late March or early April. During these months hedgerows and coverts are at their lowest, enabling ground quarry to be spotted easily by both bird and handler. Game will be in season, whilst the weather is at its coolest (see Appendix I), which avoids heat stress in a hard-hunting hawk. For these reasons, there is little point in a hunting bird being asked to pursue quarry much after March, when cover is becoming high, as it will simply struggle to see a bolting rabbit running along a hedgerow, for instance. It would also be difficult, if not impossible, to locate one's bird in a tree when it is in full leaf.

Towards March, therefore, the austringer should begin to think about the moult and make sure that the moulting pen, if one is to be used, is robust and suitable to house a hawk for the next five months or so. If not, repairs should be carried out immediately, for if the bird is to be allowed free flight, you will not want to carry out any maintenance work when the very intention is not to upset her unnecessarily.

Most austringers will not have the benefit of a larger moulting pen, and will have to settle for the standard weathering in which to moult out their birds. If this is the case, the area may be a little too confined to allow the hawk free flight. It may therefore be preferable for her to stay tethered throughout the moult. Although this is not ideal, there is no reason why the moult should not go smoothly, with the new feathers looking immaculate. Five or six months is, however, a rather long time for a bird to be tethered in the same area with no exercise, and boredom may easily set in, which can result in the hawk plucking her feathers. If she remains reasonably calm, she can be taken onto the weathering lawn and allowed to enjoy a bath. Another concern which could arise from moulting a hawk out tethered is foot problems due to the length of time spent on the perch. Have a variety of bows with different tops, such astroturf, rubber, cord and leather, and alternate them each week.

The moult itself is triggered by a number of environmental and physical changes, but fundamentally it is the approach of longer daylight hours and the warmer temperatures this brings. The moult will commence around March provided the austringer does not hold his charge at a tight flying weight or the bird is not ill; these two factors can substantially slow the moult or halt it altogether. One should pick the final hunting day of the season with a view to feeding the bird up, as the idea is to get her new feathers through in good time for the following, hawking season. There is therefore no logical reason to keep the bird's weight tight, as the moult will simply not start and the following season will only take longer to come around.

It takes approximately seven weeks from the time of an old feather dropping until the new one has completely grown down and hardened off. Although it is common for falconers to say their bird has 'dropped a feather', feathers do not drop off, they are pushed out by the developing new ones. Once the feather has grown fully it is dead. These old feathers should be kept safe if they are in good condition, in case one is needed for imping during the hunting season.

The concern for the falconer is always the fine completion of the vital flight feathers, the primaries, secondaries and tail feathers, as these allow the hawk to perform with skill and agility. During the growth of the feather, the quill is filled with blood, and as it grows so the blood is reduced. This is when the webbing becomes visible. At this stage the feather is extremely sensitive and if it is knocked, it may bleed or snap.

Feathers can also show signs of deformity if the bird is denied food, stressed or flown. This will be seen in pinched feathers, fret-marked feathers and feathers which show signs of hunger traces. A pinched feather is the result of the bird being upset during the new feather's growth. Fret marks appear as darkened bars running horizontally along the webbing. Again this is caused by the bird being upset and stressed. And if the bird is denied adequate amounts of food whilst moulting, the new feathers will look untidy, giving the plumage an overall appearance of scruffiness.

Through care and consideration, these deformities can easily be avoided. Should you decide to fly your bird midway through the moult, you will have a bird with the most unsightly-looking plumage. Allow her space and quietness to complete the moult and never upset her unnecessarily. Stress ought to be eliminated as much as possible, especially if she is more nervous than usual. Stress will destroy any chance of a successful moult, it can even contribute to a bird's death. Like us, a bird's skin colour will change when it is scared and stressed, although this can not be seen through the feathers. This is because of a reduction in the amount of blood going to the growing feathers, and the end result will be feathers with ugly fret marks.

Birds of prey are very much susceptible to parasites, especially when the weather is at its warmest. Mites can seriously damage a bird's plumage and one must take precautionary measures against them. Before and on completion of the moult the bird should be sprayed with Johnson's Antimite, which is an essential combating agent. Many austringers take their bird to the vets for a annual physical examination, generally on completion of the moult.

A bird of prey will do a great deal herself to maintain fine-looking plumage by preening. A preening gland situated at the base of the two centre tail feathers produces oil, which the bird uses to waterproof and shield the feathers. Bathing in water is also vital for natural feather management. The falconer can play an essential part by being thoughtful during his bird's inactivity by not upsetting her or giving her cause for panic. A hawk which has scruffy plumage does not say anything positive about the keeper, look after her plumage and help her to fly to the best of her ability.

Harris hawks and the law, past and present

by PC Paul Beecroft

During the early 1960s, when we first saw Harris hawks entering the UK from South America, there were virtually no controls on the trade in wildlife, unlike the situation today. And once the bird had arrived in the UK and was with the falconer, there were no legislative controls over the keeping of it. Birds received minimal protection under the law and what protection existed was mainly in respect of cruelty under the Protection of Animals Act 1911.

This is how it remained until a new Act came into being, the Wildlife and Countryside Act 1981. This totally changed things as far as the keeping of hawks, falcons and eagles in captivity was concerned. Under this Act all keepers were required by law to have all species of falconiformes ringed and registered. The Harris hawk was obviously included in this category. The Act was administered by what was known then as the Department of the Environment (now Department of the Environment, Transport and the Regions), based in Bristol. Not only was a ring issued for each bird but also a registration document that gave details of its origin (captive-bred, imported etc.). In the early days of the Act most Harris hawks were fitted with a cable-tie ring to identify them as in the main they were adult birds and unsuitable for closed rings. The captive breeding of Harris hawks in this country was quite successful by this time, and therefore most chicks being hatched were fitted with closed rings.

Once this system was truly up and running there were a lot of benefits to it. The registration document was able to provide details of the bird such as its age and the parents' ring numbers. It also went a long way to help keepers show that the bird was legally owned. It was not by any means 100 per cent foolproof, and it was never intended to be, but it did do a great deal in helping both the keeper and the authorities to check the legalities of the bird.

Under the provisions of the Act, it was an offence to keep a bird of prey which was not ringed and registered. Keepers convicted of this offence paid a heavy penalty and could end up being banned from keeping a bird of prey for three or five years depending on the species concerned. In the case of the Harris hawk it was three years.

This system was especially helpful in reducing theft, especially of Harris hawks, which by this time had become very popular for falconry. The price of a Harris hawk ran into many hundreds of pounds at that time, and the theft of birds of prey was not uncommon. The ringing and registration scheme was not introduced for this reason, but it did reduce the number of birds being stolen from captivity. Birds, once stolen, usually had to have their rings removed, for obvious reasons. It was then not always an easy job to re-enter the bird into the registration scheme as questions would be asked as to its origin etc. Thieves would therefore have to keep these hidden. A number of people were caught this way and even if the authorities could not prove that the birds were stolen the persons concerned were convicted of ringing and registration offences and subjected to the normal penalty.

The system worked well for the next ten years, and most keepers of birds of prey were happy with it. It afforded some protection, not only for the birds but for the keeper himself. It also, I believe, gave some respectability to falconry and showed the general public that our birds were being kept legally and that we were subject to strict controls and liable to spot inspections.

However, in 1993, the Department of the Environment announced a review of the Wildlife and Countryside Act 1981, and the ringing and registration scheme was to be one of the main points included in this review. Figures were presented showing that the number of birds of prey being held in captivity had increased considerably over the past ten years, from an estimated 1500 at the commencement of the Act to 16,000 specimens in 1992. The Government believed that the time had come to reduce substantially the number of birds required to be ringed and registered. Wild populations of many species had increased since 1981, in particular the kestrel, common buzzard and sparrowhawk. This was of course true, but at the same time these birds had the highest percentage of prosecutions for not being ringed and registered. Also, non-native birds were not free-living in Britain and therefore could not be taken from the wild, hence a substantial number of these could also be removed from the Act. From figures supplied in 1992 it was known that there was a total of 1815 Harris hawks registered in this country. The kestrel had the highest number, with 3855. Emphasis was placed on how much it cost to operate the registration scheme and many people believed that it was now too expensive to manage.

In May 1994 the changes were implemented and the Harris hawk, along with many other species, was removed from the provisions of the Act in respect of ringing and registration. Just prior to this then immediately afterwards the theft of birds of prey from captivity rocketed. A staggering 200 per cent rise was recorded in the first year. Species that had never been stolen before, such as the tawny eagle, African goshawk, red-headed merlin and sooty falcon, were now being targeted by thieves. The Harris hawk, being the most popular falconry bird, was soon established as the most popular bird to steal as well.

It was now permissible to keep these birds openly without them being ringed, and all the thief had to do, therefore, was remove the ring and all history of the bird was virtually gone. Another aspect that was lost to falconers and keepers was the very effective lost-and-found service that the Department of the Environment were able to provide. Any bird lost and then found was soon returned to the owner because records showed who he was. This service, for a large number of species, has now gone. Although there are two very good privately run lost-and-found organisations, Raptor Lifeline and the Independent Bird Register, they do not have access to records. Since 1994, over 100 Harris hawks have been reported lost and never been found. One wonders of course how many of these have consequently been stolen.

There was still some limited protection for the Harris hawk in respect of sales and its use for commercial purposes. The legislation in respect of this was the Convention on International Trade in Endangered Species (CITES), whose aim is to regulate the trade in species listed in the appendices to the convention. At the time all falcons and hawks were either what were known as Appendix I species or were classified as CI to Appendix II. The Harris hawk was a CI species. CITES is implemented throughout the EU by European regulations, and the legislation which gives force to this is the Control of Trade in Endangered Species (Enforcement) Regulations 1985, known as COTES. Under Article 6 of Regulation (EEC) No 3626/82 it was an offence to sell and display any species listed in Appendix I or CI unless the conditions of a General Licence Exemption could be met. This exemption was known as EC CITES EX/36 and some of the conditions that applied were as follows:

- The bird must have been bred in captivity. A bird was not regarded as bred in captivity unless its parents were lawfully in captivity when the egg from which it hatched was laid. Documentary evidence of captive breeding must accompany any sale.
- The bird must be ringed with a legible individually numbered metal close ring, which is a ring or band in a continuous circle (without any break or join) which has not been tampered with in any way and which cannot be removed from the bird when its leg is fully grown.
- The owner of any bird to be sold under such a licence was required, if requested by an official of the Department of the Environment or police officer, to make the bird available for a sample of blood to be taken from the bird to be sold. The blood sample would be taken by a qualified veterinary surgeon. Such a sample could be used to establish the ancestry of the bird.

As can been seen this legislation assisted in ensuring that all birds being sold were legitimate. No bird could be legally sold without a closed ring and some form of document had to be provided stating that the bird was lawfully bred in captivity. This without doubt assisted the buyer in proving that the bird was legal. It also assisted the authorities in back-tracking a bird through different owners should the need arise.

On 1 June 1997, EC Regulation 338/97 came into force, replacing regulation 3626/82. This regulation changed the controls concerning the sale, display etc. of many birds of prey. Under this new regulation, which was forced on us by other EU countries, species of fauna and flora were divided into four annexes, A–D. For bird of prey annexes A and B are the relevant ones; only one bird of prey is included in Annex D. Under this regulation strict sales and purchase controls were introduced for all species included on Annex A. The Harris hawk, together with a number of other species including the redtail however, was excluded. From this date, all legislation for the Harris hawk was lost. These birds can now be freely sold, displayed and owned without any need for ringing or any documentation whatsoever. There is now no difference between the sale of a Harris hawk and a domestic cat. One might argue that this is good; after all, there is already a lot of legislation in respect of birds of prey – many believe, too much. I have to wonder, though, why this species was left off Annex A when other non-indigenous species are included.

Security

Year after year after year, bird theft is on the increase. One would think by now that falconers would be wise to this fact and protect their possessions in such a way as to reduce the risks of theft to the absolute minimum.

Following deregistration in the mid-1990s, the theft of birds was quickly on the increase and species which were once never targeted were soon being snatched. It appears that the keepers and breeders of Harris hawks are at higher risk than most, as these are the birds most frequently taken; as we have seen well over 100 have been stolen over the past three years alone.

Some years ago my own premises were broken into and a number of falcons removed from their weatherings. The feeling that one experiences when this happens is beyond words, but I can tell you it was a very distressing time indeed. Just the thought that somebody had entered my premises uninvited and helped themselves to the birds which I had worked so hard to purchase, care for and train left a feeling of total numbness, a feeling which I hope as few bird keepers as possible will ever go through.

Once I had assessed the extent of the break-in, I immediately contacted my local police and then PC Paul Beecroft at Thames Valley Police. After my call to Paul, I was left feeling even more distressed, as it was apparent that I had done very little to protect my birds, simply putting bolts on the aviary doors. The vast majority of austringers will protect their weatherings from intruders such as foxes, but rarely give theft a second thought.

The birds which were stolen from me were also my display birds, which meant my livelihood. Without the birds I had minimal income. The summer months are the busiest for display work and my break-in occurred shortly before I was to take up the birds and start retraining.

Needless to say I let a lot of committed clients down and my income suffered drastically as I had no alternative but to cancel approximately half of my bookings.

It is quite simple to gain entry into a weathering. Most are constructed from wooden fence panels and contain a large wire-fronted area. The door is rarely reinforced, which is rather stupid, as it is the most obvious entry point; some weatherings do not even have a lock. But one can do so much, both in deterring and in preventing theft with a little thought and imagination.

Having learnt the hard way, I was going to make quite sure that should an attempt ever again be made on my stock, the thief would not find the going easy. I took heed of some basic security advice from Paul Beecroft and began by checking all the hinges of the doors, making sure the screws were securely tightened. I changed the locks to the type which is toughened, making them extremely difficult to be bolt-cropped. I dug a one metre pathway, which I filled with gravel, along the entire frontage of the weatherings. Although the noise of someone walking on this path would be unlikely to wake me during the night, the crunching would certainly alert my dogs whose barking would.

The next deterrent was to fix a security night light high up on a wall, making sure it could not easily be knocked out. Although this light would react unnecessarily to inquisitive foxes, I could live with this, but another theft would be extremely difficult. To finish off my security measures, I attached a dummy CCTV system that had a built-in LED light. Although the system did not contain any film, any thief 'casing' my premises was not to know this. Many years later I am glad to say that I have not had any recurrences and I have now purchased a proper alarm system and a real surveillance TV system.

Obviously the best security measure is an alarm system. Unfortunately they are quite expensive. If a system is within your means, however, then I would recommend that you purchase one. An alternative measure, which I used until I could afford a proper alarm system, was a flashing LED light. These small units are intended for vehicles and sit on the dashboard. I bought one for each weathering and screwed them in the best internal position. Just before dark, they would be switched on and the bright red light flickered on and off throughout the night. I was sure that this would prove to be an excellent deterrent, as no one could be totally confident that it was not in fact a real alarm system. They cost approximately £5 from most car assessory shops, making them a cost-effective piece of apparatus.

Once you have been a victim, it is easy to become over-cautious, possibly to the point of being ridiculous. But as the saying goes, once bitten. My birds were taken during the evening, which is when one might expect a theft to be carried out, but I was surprised to learn that many bird thefts take place during the day, which I find even more alarming. It seems that the modern thief is bolder and greedier than ever.

(o) *Ami feeding from the fist*

(p) *Ami closing in on a kill*

(q) Hawking from horseback

(r) Ami in adult plumage

In addition to the above measures, it is also wise to be careful what you tell people, especially those with whom you are not totally familiar. Discussing your collection of birds with anybody who is not known as a trustworthy friend is foolish. Paul Beecroft once told me that victims of bird theft nearly always knew the guilty party. The average thief is now an expert. They know which birds are valuable and which are not worth bothering with. In my case, from approximately twenty birds, the target was only the falcons, in other words the most valuable. It would have to have been someone with a knowledge of raptors who committed this sordid act. I have heard alarming stories of breeders having an entire pen wiped out. Not only are the adult birds stolen, but also the young that they are rearing. The average person would be very wary of going into a pen of adults rearing offspring, which shows that these people know exactly how to handle a potentially aggressive situation. From this, one may conclude that it could be other raptor keepers that are the guilty ones.

Look at your premises from a thief's point of view and scrupulously take measures to make his task as difficult as possible. Keep as low a profile as possible and try not to advertise the fact that birds of prey are kept on the premises. This is often impossible, but the fewer people who know, the less chance there will be of a break-in.

Having a dog outside in a kennel is certainly a good deterrent and it may be all you will ever need, although not every dog will bark at an intruder. Make sure your dog is reliable enough to let you know that something is awry. At the time of my break-in my dog, who would normally be living outside in a kennel, was on loan to a friend. This may have been the reason why I was hit when I was; I think most thieves would be wary if there was a dog around.

Just as upsetting as having my birds stolen was the thought that whoever now has them may not have the knowledge and ability to look after them. Like most raptor owners, I try to keep my birds in the very highest order, caring for them and feeding them properly. It is a worrying thought that they may be being fed on unsuitable food or mishandled. For those birds which are mid-way through their moult, the stress could affect their growing feathers. Moreover, we are all too aware that stress can easily kill a bird. Even an eyass travelling home from the breeder in suitable conditions can keel over and die.

With so many worries, it is common sense to do everything in one's power to prevent theft. Owning a bird of prey is a big enough responsibility for those who know the bird and have a good knowledge of falconry. For the thief, who may have little or no knowledge, looking after the bird until it is re-homed must be all but impossible.

Bird theft concerns us all and it must be eliminated as far as possible. My advice to any austringer purchasing a bird of prey which does not come directly from the breeder is to pick it up from the seller's home. Never meet at a lay-by or motorway service area, for if the bird is a Harris hawk no paperwork is required from the seller and you may be purchasing a stolen bird. If everyone followed this advice, maybe the message would get through to the criminal element, who would then be reluctant to risk stealing a bird, knowing that no one, except other criminals, would be prepared to purchase a bird in suspicious circumstances.

If you do have any birds stolen, immediately contact your local police station. An officer will call at your premises to inspect the situation and ask some questions. Think of anybody that you have noticed loitering around you premises, or anyone you have spoken to who may have been asking probing questions; maybe someone called some weeks ago in response to an advert offering a bird for sale. Think of anything which might give the police something to go on. Also, give the officer information about the bird's ring numbers, species and gender.

Something else which you may like to keep in mind is that a thief may well come back the very next night to take more of your stock. When I was told this, my defences were on red alert and I watched my premises intensely throughout the following week.

I would recommend all austringers to register their birds with the Independent Bird Register, whose details can be found on page 142. The organisation has a central computer which is linked to police stations, falconry centres, zoos and veterinary surgeries etc. The IBR has reunited many stolen or lost birds with their rightful owners. In fact, they once found a sakret of mine that went AWOL, for which I am eternally grateful.

Bird theft is a callous crime which must be stopped. We can begin by making our weatherings as robust as possible then use physical and material deterrents. If you do not have a dog, think about purchasing one. Be careful what you say to people that you are not familiar with. And finally, do not purchase any bird which you feel is suspicious. Make sure you are up to date with current legislation and if ever in any doubt contact the Department of the Environment, Transport and the Regions.

LOOKING AHEAD

Is the Harris hawk the bird for you?

Occasionally, one will hear experienced austringers saying the Harris hawk does not make a good beginner's bird. Such people believe that they are so easily trained that the beginner will have learnt very little. I totally disagree. Those who hold this opinion are usually falconers who have been involved in the sport for many many seasons, and are accomplished people who will probably be flying goshawks or falcons. I find their views hard to accept, as nothing to do with falconry could be classed as easy. If a beginner takes a Harris hawk through the entire training process without gaining invaluable knowledge in many key areas, then there must be something seriously wrong.

A friend once told me a story of a austringer who purchased a male Harris hawk. The bird was fully parent-reared and came from a breeder

30) Ami stretching her wings

of high reputation and morals. After permitting his hawk the normal settling-down time, it did little more than thrash and kick about relentlessly during early and mid-manning sessions. Even if the hawk sat on the fist for a minute or two he would immediately fall backwards, first onto his backside and then completely off the fist, to resume bating. His behaviour was more like that of a goshawk than a supposedly mild-mannered Harris hawk. After a week or so's training, the bird would, whilst on the creance, fly immediately to the fist when called, at a weight of 652 g (1 lb 7 oz). The following day, at the very same weight and time, he did little more than sit on his perch admiring everything else around him, as if oblivious of the falconer who was offering food upon the gauntlet. This irrational behaviour carried on for a couple of long-drawn-out weeks. One person advised a further cut in weight, another an increase. Both were tried but to no avail.

Another friend who acquired a female Harris hawk took her through the manning and training process with very little problem. She proved to be a relaxed bird who relished being in the falconer's company. A fault was soon evident, however, when she was set loose. She would not come back to the fist when called. As soon as she was offered food, accompanied by the whistle command she would begin tree-hopping as if in search of her own sport. This behaviour arose when the bird was slipped from the fist in pursuit of quarry. If the target was missed, instead of returning to the falconer, as Harris hawks are supposed to do, she would find a suitable vantage point and scout for quarry. From a high point in a tree she was able to zone the surrounding fields. On numerous occasions it was only telemetry which located the bird. To get her fully under control, one literally had to throw a garnished lure onto the ground and make in. Again it was only the falconer's experience, time and dedication which solved this annoying problem, as indeed was the case with the male mentioned above.

If any of the above problems had happened to a complacent beginner, who had heard so often that telemetry is not required for such a species, or that Harrises are rock steady etc., then my guess is that his bird would soon have been forgotten about as it lived a life of seclusion in its weathering.

Although one will from time to time, still see beginners starting with kestrels and buzzards, I think this is nowadays the result of bad advice or a lack of proper consideration. To some degree, the kestrel is still looked upon as a good beginner's bird, but perhaps the real reason is their low purchase price. Falconry birds are not scarce, nor are their prices frightening.

The kestrel is a very small and fragile longwing. Here at the Eagle-Owl School of Falconry we do not believe that the beginner should start with any longwing, let alone something as delicate as this. Kestrels require a professional touch consistently throughout their training to keep them flying fit. There is no room for mistakes, or the bird's health will quickly plummet. Unfortunately many of these little birds do die because the beginner is ill-equipped to establish a correct flying weight. Even if a flying weight is attained, a bird as small as this could not be classed as a serious falconry bird as the quarry which it is capable of taking is no bigger than a field vole. Nor is its prey suitable for human consumption. Many budding falconers who have attended our courses have not realised the limits of a kestrel's true capabilities. Many believe that they and barn owls have the ability to catch rabbits or even hares. When told that this would be physically impossible, and the reasons why, their faces cloud over in embarrassment. It is obvious that people just do not understand the limits of certain birds. To a degree however, it is reassuring to give such disheartening news to those attending a course as hopefully this may stop them from purchasing the bird only to then realise what a terrible mistake has been made.

Another popular beginner's bird is the common buzzard, but again, it is not entirely suited to the novice looking to pursue falconry in all its glory. Although it is a reasonably large bird, and therefore harder for an inexperienced falconer to kill when trying to establish a flying weight, the beginner may put a great deal of time into its manning and training, only to be disappointed that it is just not capable of giving variety of sport. Buzzards have often been described as lazy and lacking in enthusiasm, but I do not totally agree with this. Any hawk, no matter what its natural capabilities are, will only be as enthusiastic as the austringer. A lazy austringer, ultimately produces a lazy hawk. A buzzard, if flown regularly, and at a correct weight, will fly quarry with optimum enthusiasm. However, in terms of ability one can confidently say that it will be overshadowed by the skill and grit of the Harris hawk. This is not to say that such a species will not give one sport. There are some very capable buzzards, but a beginner who purchases a common buzzard should understand that it will be harder to handle and train, slower in flight and restricted in the quarry it is physically able to take.

Even to those who say they will start with a buzzard and move onto the Harris I would say think again. The Harris will have a far better temperament and will be more gutsy and talented in the field, giving you a greater variety of quarry to pursue. So why purchase a buzzard when one has no intention of keeping it after the training is complete? Again one wonders if the price has something to do with it.

The beginner with a high regard for his sport and the birds he uses ought to purchase a bird with the ability to take the quarry which is available over the land that is on offer. One should also take into account that it is a long-term commitment so it should be a bird that can reach your expectations. In this way perhaps we will see fewer mature birds offered for sale. Obviously all austringers will want to progress to other species and so they should. But to purchase a bird without giving the matter of why some serious thought is being irresponsible. Those who have three or four hawks, two or three falcons and a barn owl often have too many birds and will struggle to get even one flying fit. Often those with this number of birds will only have time for one or two whilst the rest just stay tethered season after season.

I think those who run down Harris hawks too easily forget that we were all beginners once with little or no hands-on experience. I clearly remember training my first falconry bird. The thought that one day he would be ready to fly free and chase quarry was one of the most daunting imaginable. The beginner who attends a falconry course and purchases his first bird will no doubt feel exactly the same. But although there can be no guarantees, should you start off with a Harris hawk then you are starting with a bird which should be easier going than any other. Do not, however, listen to those who say it will be a doddle to train, as this may lead to complacency, and in falconry there is no room for complacency

I agree that training a Harris hawk will be a different experience from training any other hawk, but this should complement the beginner's lack of knowledge. He will receive invaluable experience in key areas such as handling a large hawk, training, entering, understanding food values and, most importantly, weight control. When you have a good knowledge of these and many other skills, you can begin thinking of moving on to other species which require a much more precise touch. Until such time, I strongly believe that the Harris hawk is the bird to learn with.

It is a privilege to be invited to various falconry clubs throughout the UK. I am interested to hear other austringers' stories, to learn about the birds they are flying and to exchange views. Occasionally when I ask about the birds they are flying, the answer is often, 'Only a Harris hawk' or 'Just a Harris hawk'. Why 'only' or 'just'? Those who fly redtails or goshawks do not use these derogatory words. It is as if the austringer flying the Harris hawk is embarrassed. Why? Perhaps it is because too many experienced falconers have damned them by saying things such as true falconers do not fly Harris hawks. This is rubbish.

One culprit was a friend of mine. Here was a austringer who was dedicated to flying longwings. Most of the season would be taken up with the falcons but during the final third he would use his hawks, both Harris hawks and a goshawk. Never have I heard anyone slander the Harris as much as he did. If he was asked what birds he was flying his reply would be either the falcons or goshawk but never the Harris hawks. I asked some seasons ago if he would sell me his male Harris, to which he replied with a definite no. All of a sudden not only his male Harris but also his female were the best things since the evolution of falconry and no sum of money would see him part company with either. Could this be the very same man who ridicules the Harris hawk and those who choose to fly them. If there is a moral to this story it is that many folk just do not like to admit that they enjoy flying a Harris hawk. I have flown many Harrises during my career, just as I have accipiters and longwings, and what is more, I am proud of the fact.

In my opinion the Harris hawk is ideally suited to the beginner, and to the intermediate or experienced austringer who seeks an almost therapeutic style of hawk ownership. It is suitable for the novice for more than one reason. It is a large bird, which means it is not going to fall down dead while you are finding an optimum flying weight. Remember, the larger the bird the less likely you will be to kill her. She will also long to be in the austringer's company and readily accept his surroundings. She will show intelligence without appearing rebellious and quickly understand what is being asked of her.

The beginner should always remember that a Harris hawk will perform at a weight which is in fact too high. She may respond to the fist and both lures with the utmost keenness when in actual fact, she could do with a further drop in weight just to sharpen that killer instinct. This will, however, become apparent should she miss or decline kills that she should probably have caught. It is a fact that most beginners keep their first birds at a weight which is too high for fear of dropping them to the point where they keel over. By applying controlled, measured weight-loss tactics, a hawk as big as a Harris will not suffer greatly if her weight is reduced further than necessary. Remember the signs of a low hawk: slitty eyes, puffed-up feathers, weak bates etc.

The beginner is also advised to let his hawk progress at the pace which suits her, as boredom may easily set in otherwise. One should be aiming to take her through the training process as quickly as possible, but without rushing. The intelligence of the Harris hawk is such that if she does become bored, she may get a little vocal. Assessing a hawk's progress is, I believe, one of the hardest things for the novice to do. Under no circumstances should one be hasty and never fly your bird free until you are happy and ready yourself, but be realistic about her progress and move on to the next stage as swiftly as possible, thus keeping the training flowing.

The Harris hawk will give the austringer a great deal of sport and should be allowed to fly whatever takes her fancy. Never hold her back on a bate unless it is clear she is just being disobedient. Nor should she be allowed to specialise in one particular quarry as she has the potential and talent to fly a vast variety of fur and feather and it is the duty of the falconer to take his charge to venues where alternative quarry will be available to her.

Make no mistake of the time you will need to find throughout the year to look after your bird and maintain her in a healthy condition, thus justifying her ownership. Time and dedication are of major importance in falconry; without them both one will never make the grade. The ownership of any bird of prey is a massive challenge; do not think it is easier for those who own Harris hawks. Contrary to some opinion the Harris hawk is not a weekender's bird. The weekender's bird will always struggle to achieve and maintain fitness and will look remarkably ordinary compared to hawks being flown throughout the week. A bird of prey will only achieve proper fitness by chasing quarry regularly. Relying on weekends alone is just not good enough. My advice to those who work full time during the week is to wait until you have mid-week flexibility or else fly at night. Trying to fit flying into a full-time working schedule, although not impossible, will push your dedication to the very limit. Working full time and trying to maintain a healthy hunting hawk will never be easy. Many falconers' lives revolve around their birds – mine does, and always will. We sacrifice many things, including our income during the season, but money is no substitute for the sight of a hunting raptor pursuing its quarry.

I am often asked by beginners and intermediate falconers why so many Harris hawks are reported lost when experienced falconers have told them that they are foolproof. In every edition of the *Falconer's Magazine* there will be a section for birds lost, found and stolen, which will include many lost Harris hawks. The answer is that any bird of prey can go AWOL. I am always astounded at the number of Harris hawks on field meets which are not fitted with a radio telemetry device. This can only be for one of two reasons: either the owner cannot afford to purchase a set, or the attitude is that the bird is so steady and trustworthy it could never get lost. Again I sense an air of complacency in this view. Let us be clear: a Harris hawk, like any other hawk, has the ability to fly, hence the ability to fly away. I have known many experienced austringers who have needed to track their Harrises down for some reason. I have also known many more who have learnt of the benefits of telemetry the hard way. Do not be one of them.

Harris hawks in the future

In bygone years, a Harris hawk was, for many people, simply too expensive. During the early 1960s Harris hawks were not available to the UK falconer. In fact, in comparison with today, few species were available for falconry purposes. For this reason one would see both experienced and novice falconers restricted to birds such as goshawks, imported redtails, buzzards, sparrowhawks, kestrels, peregrines and sakers, as these were the birds which were easiest to obtain. Indeed, my own career started with a kestrel. Although I learnt a lot in terms of precise weight control, the bird, I am sure, would have died if I had not had an experienced austringer looking over my every move.

It was around 1962 that the first Harris hawks entered the UK from the USA. There were, at that time, few import restrictions or documents required, hence it was extremely easy to bring non-indigenous birds into Great Britain. But during the early 1960s, the Harris hawk was not

31) A youngster with a mature female Harris hawk

recognised as a serious falconry contender and only a dedicated few were prepared to persevere and bring out its potential, learning of its abilities both during the training and in the hunting field. Around 1968 the first captive-bred specimens hatched in the UK. People's interest in the bird started to grow, as it was around this time that it was seen publicly at flying displays such as the Country Landowners' Association's game fair. One could expect to pay approximately £400 to £500 for a Harris eyass during the late 1960s and early 1970s soaring to around £2,000 in the late 1970s.

It was during the late 1970s and early 1980s that the Harris established itself as a serious hunting companion. Never before had one been able to fly hawks in a cast, and this was highly appealing to the falconer. It was quickly realised that the bird had a relaxing temperament and was able to take a wide range of quarry, bringing the falconer additional scope. The breeders soon realised the potential for the bird, and breeding programmes became more and more common.

Those starting out in falconry are today in a completely different situation from those ten or twenty years ago. Captive breeding has brought the price of Harris hawks and many other species plummeting to within the reach of everyone's pocket. For many this is a mixed blessing, as one no longer has to think long and hard about the purchase price of a hawk.

Many other birds which have been cheap for a number of years, such as owls, have, I am sure, been exploited by undesirables looking for a new status symbol. I believe that any animal which requires specialist care should carry a price tag which makes those who are not fully committed to its management think twice before buying it. No longer does a person have to be totally confident that falconry is right for them when a bird which was once a large initial investment can be bought for very little. On the other hand however, it does allow the genuine falconer to pursue his sport with a Harris hawk and many other raptors without paying an exorbitant price.

Today's beginner is not only spoilt for choice in terms of birds, but falconry courses and suppliers are springing up all over the country and competing for business. More books and videos are available to help guide the beginner, whilst the Internet provides one with unlimited information, especially on local falconry clubs, where one can learn from those with many successful seasons behind them. This has to be a good thing for falconry, as there is now no excuse for the novice not acquiring the correct knowledge and skill to be successful. With all these possibilities one is well equipped to get onto the first rung of the ladder and enjoy falconry to the full.

During my research for this book, many falconers expressed some concern about inbreeding. Since deregistration, inbreeding has been a major threat to Harris hawks. Because of their popularity, it is very difficult to keep track of those brought together for the purposes of breeding. Many people fear that in years to come this will result in a drop in popularity as potential purchasers are put off by the fear that they might acquire an inbred bird that could show signs of illness. Unfortunately, there is currently very little which can be done to guarantee that two birds in a breeding aviary are not related. Hopefully breeders will address this issue now and keep detailed notes of their stock. And looking through specialist magazines, one finds some Harris hawk breeders who do state that the youngsters offered for sale are from unrelated stock.

Provided that we do not encounter large-scale problems with inbreeding, and that all breeders show the necessary diligence when matching together pairs, I think the Harris hawk will continue to be as popular in years to come just as it is now, as pound for pound no other hawk will give one the same level of consistent sport day in and day out.

Progressing to other species

It is extremely difficult to write about the temperament of a particular species, as each bird within a species is so different from the next. All birds have their own minds and their own unique ways of thinking. Animals are just like humans: some are fat, others thin, some are tall, others small, some are highly intelligent, others a little slower. Some hawks like to bath, some do not, just like humans. Because of this individuality, all one can ever hope to do is give a general overview of a particular species derived from personal experience and talking to other austringers. In this way I hope to give as clear an account as possible of the species being discussed, although this should not be regarded as definitive.

With the variety of birds now on offer, falconry is more exciting than ever before. It is therefore natural that people should want to try their talents on those of other species. Perhaps after a season or two gaining the much needed experience with a Harris hawk, one might acquire a bird with a different flight pattern and greater potential in different areas. The choice for many people in this situation would probably be the goshawk, although changing from a Harris hawk to a goshawk would be somewhat of a culture shock. I believe that a season flying a common buzzard or red-tail will far better equip the austringer to deal with a bird such as the goshawk. Therefore those who have learnt the basics of weight control and hawk management with a Harris hawk may be better off moving on to a redtail, and gaining another perspective on training etc. before trying one of the trickiest hawks there is. And those who have served their apprenticeship on the common buzzard may find themselves better equipped in dealing with a goshawk, as their temperaments are not too dissimilar.

In all its splendour, the goshawk will give you hawking of the highest order, providing that it is flown four or five times a week every week throughout the season. Many austringers who have moved on to this species would never again fly a Harris hawk. Many reasons are given but the most frequent are its speed, excitement and ability to catch quarry such as pheasant in flight. There is no argument that the goshawk is the fastest hawk in the world. The speed they generate is quite extraordinary and if fit, an amazing sight to see.

Many of my goshawk-flying friends take great excitement from not knowing how their bird will perform from one day to the next. Unlike the Harris, the goshawk will often not return to the fist at distance, and some will not return to the fist at all. A good friend of mine who flies a mature male will see his bird fly to the fist one day and only to the lure the next. Many a night has been spent out trying to coax the bird from a tree, often with no success. In fact, his bird has frequently been missing for anything up to three days. Although this untrustworthy behaviour will not suit every austringer, there is great pleasure in watching him chase quarry with such speed, grit and determination, and this outweighs all his disadvantages. To witness a hawk fly a rabbit, miss, and land, only to regain momentum and finally catch it is quite literally astounding, and a talent which only a fit flying goshawk has. Without doubt, it is a feat of excellence.

Flying such a species will certainly give the austringer greater scope on slips. Ami, for instance, would be unable to catch a pheasant in flight as, no matter how fit she is, she just would not have the necessary speed. Like any Harris, she will attempt a runner or take the opportunity if she is in a tree and the pheasant is hiding in the cover directly below, but this is not a particularly spectacular feat.

One's expectations of a juvenile goshawk, however, should not be too high. As with all immatures, there is a great deal of learning to be done. The austringer can help boost his bird's confidence factor by offering easier flights at quarry as this will also help to build fitness. One must also be aware of the fact that the goshawk has a low blood sugar level. If the hawk's weight drops too low or too abruptly, it many throw a fit. One must be totally competent in reducing weight, as a fitting bird can end up as a dead bird.

Providing you are able to dedicate the time to get your bird fit and in good condition then I am sure you will find that a goshawk will live up to its reputation. However, if lack of time is a problem then the goshawk is certainly not the bird for you and you would be advised to leave well alone. Remember, it is impossible to over-man a goshawk.

If you feel that you do not have the ability required to own a goshawk, then the redtailed buzzard may well be worth considering. Personally I have a true passion for the redtail; I find it gives me almost everything I require from a day's hawking. The first thing you will notice, if you have previously been flying a Harris or a common buzzard, is the immense power of the redtail. For this reason I feel that it is not suited to younger or inexperienced handlers. With such a large hawk, with that sort of strength, it is vital that she is fully parent-reared for if not, you have a time bomb just waiting to go off. An imprinted redtail can do the austringer severe physical damage, especially when he is attempting to claim quarry from it. I have seen a bird strike an austringer on the top of his head, causing a nasty wound. I have also been present when a redtail has embedded its talons deep in the side of a friend's face, coming to within a fraction of leaving him permanently blind. An imprint will also be vocal.

Weather permitting, it is wise to handle and fly a redtail every day to maximise and maintain fitness and to keep a check on her temperament. Once fully fit she should be encouraged to take on harder slips, proving that she has the substance to give one serious sport. Like all hawks, she must be shown a variety of quarry, as if she is slipped on rabbit alone she may be inclined to blank feathered game when it is well within her capability.

Redtails are often thought to be sticky-footed (gripping the glove in excitement and making it difficult for a fast, *smooth* slip) in their early days, but in my opinion they are no more so than any other hawk and many which I have trained have not been sticky-footed at all. Like all hawks there is a great deal of early learning to be done but once they are flying free with their confidence high, they will waste no time chasing a variety of quarry. Those who persevere with their juvenile bird, will see them improve year after year.

The redtail is a gutsy bird which will crash into cover and attempt to charge through it. What it lacks in speed it makes up for in aggression. On many occasions my redtail has hit cover so hard I have stood off, expecting the worse. One memorable slip which springs to mind was a flight on a rabbit. My bird was in pumping flight and gaining on its prey with every wing-beat. Just as the rabbit hit light cover the hawk threw out a foot and grabbed its target by the hindquarters. On racing over, I found that it had one foot firmly gripped to its prey, whilst the other was repeatedly striking it around the head area. The strength and aggression was quite unbelievable.

Successful captive breeding has been kind to this bird and many more are now seen on organised field meetings. Redtails are competent in woodland, follow on obediently and, if encouraged, will slop soar in breathtaking style. The austringer who is dedicated to his juvenile will have the making of a solid, hungry field competitor.

Some austringers soon get the urge to fly longwings, but to achieve any results one has to be absolutely fully committed. You will need ample time on your hands to keep your bird flying fit and also have access to suitable land over which to fly her. Because of these two factors very few austringers can justify owning such birds. Many find it hard enough acquiring land to fly a Harris hawk or redtail over; it will certainly prove much harder for falcons. But for those who have the time, the money and the land, this is probably the most exciting aspect of falconry.

It appears that longwing flyers are now buying more and more hybrids – peregrine × saker, peregrine × lanner and peregrine × gyr to name but a few. Only on rare occasions do I now see straight peregrines, whilst other falcons such as lanners, sakers and luggers are now mainly reserved for flying demonstrations. They are unable to compete in terms of ability with the peregrine or peregrine hybrid, although they can give one good sport in, for example, hedgerow hawking, where the lanner can excel. If you would like to move onto longwings then you should attend a course which is dedicated solely to their manning and training.

As I have said, it is important to fly and acquaint oneself with different species, but it is also vital that any bird you buy is purchased for the right reasons. Unless your stock is moulting or in for breeding you owe it to them to see that they are all regularly exercised. Should you have too big a collection, everything will become a chore. Falconry is meant to be enjoyable, which is impossible if you have bitten off more that you can chew. You may be loaned a hawk for a season. Austringers welcome such opportunities with open arms as they give them the chance to learn about the bird and tend to it without any long-term commitment. All austringers should try alternative forms of hawking and experience the thrills which each will give. Some are content flying a Harris hawk season after season, others move on to longwings. Then there are those who devote half a season to their falcons and the other half to their hawks. Within time we all soon realise which style of hawking we prefer.

Ami in her second season

All in all I had been extremely happy with the sport Ami had given me the previous season. It had been a stress-free period as she exhibited the pleasant characteristics I have come to expect from the Harris hawk. Together we had attended some memorable field meetings and we had by no means been put to shame by those who were flying mature Harrises, redtails or goshawks. Ami had given me a solid and consistent season, and one which will stay in my memory like so many others.

Before she was put down for her moult, I decided to enter her on squirrel. I felt she had matured adequately both physically and mentally, and now knew how best to use her deadly feet to optimum effect, as she always attempted to hit her target towards the head. She had also taken over a dozen rats, which should be to her advantage.

I took her into some woodland which held an abundance of grey squirrel and let her loose. This also gave me a chance to assess her following-on aptitude, although I did not push this aspect fully until this second season. Ami took to something high up a tree and set off in hot pursuit. She weaved and turned, trying to grab her target as she did so, but the squirrel was fast, agile, fit and, from what I could see, well nourished. Ami eventually lost enthusiasm so I recalled her to the fist. Once she had regained her breath, she was up again. She followed me through the mass of large trees, although one eye was always on movement which might provide a meal. She spotted another squirrel and gave chase. It was important that she should make an early kill, as if she was consistently outmanoeuvred she might begin to think that this variety of quarry was not within her capabilities. She was frantically corkscrewing an old oak, giving all she had, trying harder than ever to make contact. Finally, through sheer grit and determination she connected with both feet, one secured on the head the other on the chest. Squirrel number one had been caught with precision and authority.

By the end of the season, she had been successful a further four times. Although many more eluded her, the joy for me was purely in the pursuit, and I was looking forward to more squirrel hawking the next season.

Throughout her first major moult, Ami remained tethered and isolated from anything which could cause her stress. This resulted in her delicate growing feathers being immaculate. I would have preferred her to have been free-lofted throughout this period, but it just was not possible at the time, due to limited aviary space. She did, however, spend a great deal of time on the weathering lawn enjoying her bath-time under her favourite

'32) Ami relaxing
vith Gypsy prior to
ier first major moult

tree, which allowed me to keep her bay fresh and clean. Most raptors, Harrises included, tend to go a little wild at fat weight and will not welcome the falconer in or even around their living quarters without excessive bating and even screaming. Should this be the case then only handle the bird when absolutely necessary or the end result may be damaged feathers.

Throughout the moult, Ami's diet consisted of little other than rodents and quail. Fresh drinking water was always available, although rarely did she accept it. One constantly needs to check the water as one does not want the bird drinking if she has muted in it beforehand.

During the close season I carried out all the daily health and safety checks both to her and to her equipment, but with less physical contact than usual, to minimise stress.

By the following September, Ami's new plumage was in perfect condition and she appeared to be in tip-top health. Soon I would need to put her on the scales to register a new fat weight, although I was not in any great rush to get her retrained as cover was still very high and many of my colleagues' hawks were still completing their moult. It was towards the end of September, just as the weather was beginning to get a little cooler that I decided to establish a new fat weight. I carefully took Ami into the weighing room and positioned her on the scales. Her weight was recorded at 1049 g (2 lb 5 oz), slightly heavier than her fat weight as an eyass.

It is a fine feeling to know that one's bird will not have forgotten all the lessons and experiences of the previous season, and that she should be flying free and in action in a fraction of the time. Although the process of manning and training in the second season will be almost identical to that when the bird was in her first year, rapid progress should be made, as the aim is to get her once again flying free and flying fit.

First, however, Ami had to be cast within a soft towel for a thorough physical examination. I took a close look at her plumage for any broken, bent or muted feathers. If any had been apparent, imping, straightening and cleaning would have had to be be carried out immediately. Next, I made a visual inspection of her legs and feet just to make sure that there were no scabs, swellings or unfamiliar discolouring. She was to be fitted with new anklets so the old ones were cut off to allow for a better inspection. Happily, everything was fine, so I cleaned her legs with warm water before I applied baby oil to nurture the scales, which were a little on the dry side. I clipped her talons back to the right length and shaped and sharpened them, as I also did her upper mandible. New anklets and jesses were placed on each leg before a new swivel and leash were attached. I then turned her onto her chest to allow me to apply the tail mount to her centre tail feathers. It was then just a case of spraying her plumage with Johnson's Anti-mite and taking her for her annual check-up and mute test at the vet's before we began work.

Once she had been given a clean bill of health, we could commence the process of establishing a new flying weight. Instead of feeding exclusively within the confines of her weathering, from now on Ami's only means of obtaining food would be via the fist. A hawk at fat weight can go many days without eating so at this stage I knew that my coaxing would almost certainly be in vain. During the first three days she showed no interest in accepting food but on the fourth she started to look at the offering, although still she declined. Her weight on the fourth day had dropped to 978 g (2 lb 2½ oz).

On day five, and at a slightly lower weight of 957 g (2 lb 1¾ oz) her head bent downwards and reluctantly she accepted her first mouthful. On the sixth day, she weighed in at 943 g (2 lb 1¼ oz). At this weight she accepted the offering quite quickly and with some degree of enthusiasm, so I wasted little time in advancing to the next stage, which was getting her to fly from her bow the length of the leash for her reward, bypassing the lessons in stepping up onto the fist altogether as I do not find this module necessary in a hawk's second season. Although she was a little distracted, she did accomplish the task albeit with severe reservations. After a few more dismal attempts, it was obvious that she required a further cut in weight, so I made sure not to give her the volume of food that I would have done had she performed satisfactory.

On day seven her weight had dropped to 914 g (2 lb ¼ oz). This reduction sharpened her up ten-fold and she now flew to the fist, a leash length, for the first time with enthusiasm. I put her on the creance and extended the distance to 1.8 m (6 ft). Again she flew quickly and with enthusiasm. By the end of the training session progress had been rapid and Ami was flying 25 m, the full length of the creance. The next day I wanted her back amongst trees, so I took her to a different plot of land, which had a few oak trees that had died many years ago. From here I could position her on a variety of branches at different heights without fear of the creance tangling. Her weight was slightly lower than the previous day and for this exercise, Tess, my puppy springer, was now by my side. Although I would have expected her to be slow back to the fist, I was pleasantly surprised. She flew reasonably quickly, with no apparent reservations about being in this strange dog's company. She was shown both lures, which she attacked with speed. I felt she did not require a further drop in weight at least until she was asked to fly quarry.

The next day I moved on to the next stage of retraining, allowing her freedom of flight. From here I could start working on her fitness again, but without the restriction of the creance.

Once Ami had re-established full fitness, we again attended many wonderful field meetings. As usual we had our good days and our bad, but she proved to be much more of a force when taking on her prey than before and was a far better bird in terms of thinking about her chase. She had bagged me some very nice dinners, and has often been rewarded with a little more than just a head or cut from a hind leg.

Next season I shall not be flying Ami, as she is to be a gift to my partner Julia, who now has time to tend a hawk of her own. I shall be going back to my goshawk, as for some reason I miss the speed, excitement, agility, bad temper, consistent bating and inconsistent mood swings.

Final thoughts

Without doubt, both the sport of falconry and birds of prey in general are receiving increased media and public exposure. Game fairs and country shows often appear barren if there is not a bird of prey flying display team embellishing the arena throughout the day. At one such show that I attended the falconer was unexpectedly taken ill and the display had to be cancelled. Never have I heard such a clamour from the public, who demanded their money back, arguing that they had only come to see the birds flying. People really were quite perturbed and the fact was made known, most of it in an undiscerning way, to the poor stewards. Although many other events were going on in and around the arena, people find the drama of raptors and owls flying tantalising. I am sure few would have remonstrated in quite the same manner if, for instance, the ferret-racing had been called off.

People from all walks of life are mesmerised by the talents of birds of prey. The majority of admirers will never consider owning a hawk; observing them at a display is enjoyment enough. But many others will seek to become falconers. And although it is flying displays which bring falconry to the attention of the public, there is a worry, which is that our sport may be made to look easier than it actually is. Actual participants are all aware that it is one of the most demanding entertainments in the world, but people only see fit birds at displays and not the endless time, effort and commitment which the austringer will have put into each and every one. Although the good which comes from displays far outweighs any bad, I have often been concerned that a few people will see the barn owl, for instance, as a nice pet, when in fact nothing could be further from the truth. Nevertheless, I welcome the fact that displays bring people into the sport, as fresh faces will help our sport to grow and give it more credibility in society; they say there is safety in numbers.

But, as I have said, it is vital that if newcomers do wish to get involved and take on the ownership of a raptor, then it should be for the right reasons. Over the years I have learnt to divide so-called falconers into five groups (I leave it to you to decide who the true falconers actually are). First, there are those whose lives revolve around their birds and their sport. Day after day, they can be seen battling adverse weather conditions, determined to fly. These are people who are truly dedicated and get the very most from their birds and from the sport. Secondly, there are those who enjoy owning and flying a bird, although they are not too worried about her making a kill. These people will, perhaps, fly two or three days a week, providing the weather is not too cold. They will have attended a course and gained some basic training and husbandry knowledge to keep their birds in the very finest condition. Thirdly, there are those who have bought a Harris hawk but have had no formal training, learning what they can from books alone. These people will be seen once, occasionally twice a week over local parks and woodland, flying their bird with little success. They will allow their birds to kill in front of the public, which can cause outrage and give falconry bad publicity. Often their interest will be casual and they will give up after a season or two, having damaged our sport's reputation. Fourthly, there are those who have no interest in hawking. They are content to fly their hawk or owl to the fist once a week, over the park or in the back garden. These people desire nothing else from the sport. Rarely will they have had any formal training, but will have learnt what they can from books and videos alone. They end up with a number of birds, mainly owls, and may be seen carrying out static displays at fund-raising days etc. Finally, there are those who purchase a hawk as a status symbol. These individuals can often be seen walking down the road, Harris hawk on arm, relishing all the attention they receive. The least said about these people the better, I think.

A bird of prey is not an extension of one's ego, nor is it a status symbol to gain attention. It is to be respected and given the high quality of life it deserves, and used for an ancient sport or for educational and conservation purposes. If it is not, the result could be enduring damage to our sport's standing and to those of us who try to carry it out to the best of our ability. The beginner must appreciate the merits of falconry and its values, and this is where that attendance on a well structured falconry course will prove beneficial as it will give a very good grounding. It is far better to realise that falconry would not suit your current lifestyle whilst on a course and before any solid commitment and unnecessary financial outlay have been incurred, than to buy a bird, construct a weathering and purchase all the necessary equipment, only to realise then that you do not have the time to enjoy the sport as it was intended. Early recognition of these and many other factors is better for you and for the bird.

Do not attempt to learn solely from books and videos. Few beginners are lucky enough to know a practising falconer personally so one may be inclined to gain information the easiest and cheapest way. But if you want to progress in the right way and benefit from falconry then you must attend a well-run course. If the price tag puts you off, then forget falconry altogether, as you will never be able to afford a bird of prey and all the initial and ongoing expenses that come with owning it.

One year we had a student who attended a three-day course. He told me that he had saved for many weeks to pay for those few days, and that there was no way that he could afford to buy a bird of his own. His philosophy, however, was to attend a course and then join a club where he would be around raptors and falconers. By attending their field meetings, he might have a chance to fly a club bird. He could practise the many basic skills which he was about to learn on the course and the following year, once he had bought all the necessary equipment and constructed a suitable weathering, he would purchase a redtail buzzard. This man had obviously put a great deal of thought into his strategy, and I can tell you that he did acquire a redtail and is now a very competent falconer and enjoying the sport to the full.

Today's beginner is in a rather favoured position. Never before have so many helpful books and videos been available, and never before have there been so many organisations running courses. Equipment suppliers are abundant, and more and more clubs are accessible to help and guide those who wish to be a part of this rewarding pursuit. But whilst books and videos are extremely helpful, as I have said, they are unable to answer individuals' specific questions and are no substitute for a falconry course. Here you will receive professional guidance from people who have not only been participating for many years, but who are experienced and proficient in all departments.

Before booking a course, the beginner must make sure that it covers the aspects which he regards as most important. A course will not be cheap so you should be sure the tutoring deals with those key areas. After all, the intention is that you should be skilled enough upon completion to own a bird of prey, train her and get her hunting. It would be foolhardy to pay for a course and then feel let down because it did not cover your own particular needs. Most falconry schools are committed to excellence and endeavour to offer the best possible service, but I have also known of individuals who have only been practising falconers themselves for a few years and set up in business teaching others. This is alarming, as it means the next cohort of falconers would not have been taught as thoroughly as they should have been. No one could be competent enough to set up shop after just a few years. Falconry is such a complex sport that no one can ever fully understand all its many specialised areas. I have been around raptors for over twenty years and still I feel I know only a fraction of what there is to know. For me, however, this is one of the sport's appeals. One never stops learning – unless one chooses to.

As a person who teachs falconry to others, I am always trying to develop my teaching ability. This is a very important skill, which all instructors should possess, but which may be given little or no thought. The ability to teach well is difficult to master, but incompetence in this area will inevitably reflect onto the students. One may be a gifted austringer but that does not mean one has the ability to relay information clearly to others. If you do not have the ability to teach, and to assess each student individually so that you recognise any weak areas which need further explaining, then shyer students will remain confused. It is very easy to tell people to say if anything is unclear, but not everyone does.

It is important to us that our students are treated as individuals, as each will have his own needs. Some grasp the tying of the falconer's knot within minutes, others take all day and some do not manage it at all. There are those who are very worried about weight control whilst others take it in their stride. Everyone is different. For these and other reasons all our courses are carried out on a one-to-one basis. If we took more, I think we would struggle to give each one enough of our personal time.

From a teaching point of view I believe the most important point to emphasise to a student is the time and commitment that will have to be found for the bird. This is required on a daily basis for as long as the bird is in one's possession. The ownership of a raptor is extremely time-consuming even for those of us who make a living from their keeping, so for those who work full time I have nothing but admiration. Moreover, it is inevitable that a bird will require specialist veterinary attention at some time or other. This is never cheap, and is something which must be thought about before a hawk is purchased. Avian medicine has come on in leaps and bounds over the years, and modern techniques and drugs can quickly turn a declining bird's life around. The beginner contemplating hawk ownership must therefore take all these points – cost, time and commitment – seriously, as complacency may well end your hawking days even before they have begun.

The many skills which the beginner needs will take innumerable seasons to require. One cannot be an expert in falconry and related matters after a season or two; its different facets are just too complicated. What is important is that all students are taught clearly and correctly, and that their careers begin with the right information. Those of us who provide this are in a very important position.

Those who choose to pursue falconry in all its glory must realise that it is a sport that will push their ability to the very limit. Be prepared for many disappointments throughout your career, and learn from your mistakes. Those who choose to start correctly (by attending a falconry course) will soon be a part of a wonderful sport, meet many interesting people, visit some breathtaking countryside and be rewarded with memorable flights and a feeling of ultimate achievement.

Throughout the writing of this book it was my intention to give a thorough insight into the captive-bred Harris hawk, its way of thinking, its physical ability, its good and bad points, its capabilities etc. One story which in my opinion sums all this up, especially the bird's intelligence, was e-mailed to me by my friend Adrian Williams, Secretary of the Hawking Club. It read:

> I took my female Harris hawk out one September's evening, just a couple of yards from my house. Walking into a field and towards a large greying rock I was, from this point, able to view down over a large rolling field where, as suspected, were four rabbits lying out approximately 150 yards from the nearest cover. She might take one of these, I thought. Expecting the hawk to fly straight at them she instead leaned forward and dropped off the glove to land upon the rock. The distant rabbits obviously sensed this movement because they ran directly towards a cluster of nettles. 'You idiot' was my reaction to the utter stupidity of the bird. My goshawk would have flown straight at them I thought. OK, it would not have made the distance before the rabbits made the cover, but it would have at least tried. With the rabbits now in the cover, the Harris hawk left the rock, and whilst I expected her to fly towards them – even though I knew it was now too late – she in fact rose into the air, at the same time making ground towards their hiding place. Again I murmured, 'You idiot,' as I expected a more direct flight. 'Now what?' When she was approximately 100 ft above the cover which contained the rabbits, she dropped like a stone and . . . well the rest is history. But no goshawk would have ever thought of doing it that way, hey?

This is just one of many stories I have kindly been sent, but what a story it is. Successful hawking to you all.

GAME SEASON CHART

Game species	Start of season	End of season
Pheasant*	1 October	1 February
Partridge*	1 September	1 February
Grouse*	12 August	10 December
Blackgame*	20 August	10 December
Ptarmigan*	12 August	10 December
Capercaillie	1 October	31 January
Common snipe*	12 August	31 January
Woodcock*		
England and Wales	1 October	31 January
Scotland	1 September	31 January
Duck and goose		
Inland	1 September	31 January
Foreshore above high-water		
mark of ordinary spring tides	1 September	20 February
Coot and moorhen	1 September	31 January
Golden plover	1 September	31 January
Curlew	1 September	31 January
Hare*	No close season	

Species marked with * require a game licence, available from a post office, which is renewable annually.

APPENDIX II

FALCONRY TERMS

Accipiter A true hawk with a long tail, lightly coloured eyes and short, rounded wings.
Austringer A keeper of broadwinged and shortwinged hawks.
Bate Attempt to fly off when on the glove or tethered to a perch.
Bind Hold prey securely by the feet.
Broadwing A hawk with a broad, rounded wing pattern.
Carry An attempt to fly off with prey.
Cast (noun) Two birds flown at the same time.
Cast (verb) (1) Hold a bird securely for equipping for imping and coping.
(2) Regurgitate fur, bones and feathers of food.
(3) Throw a hawk off the fist to get it airborne.
Casting A pellet containing fur, bones and feathers.
Cere The skin above and around the beak.
Condition, in At the bird's proper flying weight.
Coping Maintenance of the beak and talons.
Crines Hair around the cere.
Crop (noun) (1) The containing area, for food before it reaches the stomach.
(2) Volume of food given to the hawk at a single meal.
Deck feathers The two centre feathers of the tail.
Diurnal Hunting during the day.
Enter Give a hawk the initial flight at quarry.
Eyass A young hawk from the nest.
Falconer One who trains raptors to hunt.
Falconry The art of training raptors to hunt.
Flight feathers The main feathers used for flight.
Hack An eyass which flies free before being trained.
Hard penned Used to describe new feathers which have hardened off.
Hood shy Used to describe a hawk which resists being hooded.
Hybrid A hawk bred from two different species.
Imping The repairing of damaged feathers.
Imprint A hawk which is not parent-reared.
Intermewed Moulted in captivity.
Keen Quick in responding to the fist.
Longwing A bird with long, pointed wings.

Mail A hawk's breast feathers.

Make in Approach a hawk on a kill.

Manning The process of taming a hawk.

Mantle Try to hide prey or food beneath low spread wings.

Moult The process of dropping old feathers to make way for new ones.

Mutes A bird's faeces.

Nares A hawk's nostrils.

Passage hawk A hawk in juvenile plumage which is caught on migration.

Pitch (noun) The waiting-on height of a hawk.

Pitch (verb) Land in a tree, on the ground etc.

Plumage A bird's feathers.

Preen Clean and maintain the feathers.

Primaries The longest feathers on the wings.

Quarry The prey at which a hawk is flown.

Rouse Shake the plumage.

Secondaries The wing feathers between the hawk's body and the primaries.

Self-hunting A hawk which goes off in search of quarry of her own accord.

Serve Put quarry out of cover for a hawk.

Shortwing An accipiter or true hawk.

Slip Release a hawk from the fist in pursuit of prey.

Soar Glide on thermals, as opposed to flying at prey.

Stoop The fast flight of a longwing from a great height.

Tarsus A hawk's leg between hock and foot.

Tiercel A male peregrine.

Train A hawk's tail.

Wait on Wait overhead for quarry to be produced.

Weathering ground An area for tethering birds.

CLUBS AND ASSOCIATIONS

The British Falconers' Club
c/o John R. Fairclough
Home Farm
Hints
Nr Tamworth
Staffordshire   B78 3DW
Tel/fax: 01543 481737

The British Hawking Association
c/o Paul Beecroft (chairman)
7 Arnside Close
Twyford
Berkshire   RG10 9BS
Tel/fax: 0118 9016990
e-mail: raptorlife@aol.com
Website: www.bhassoc.org

The Hawking Club
c/o Adrian Williams
Maendy Farmhouse
Church Village
South Wales   CF38 1SY
Tel/fax: 01443 206333

The Northern England Falconry Club*
c/o D. Chadwick
31 Northorpe Lane
Mirfield
West Yorkshire   WF14 OQJ

The Scottish Hawking Club*
c/o Andrew Knowles-Brown
Crookedstane Elvanfoot
By Biggar
Lanarkshire   ML12 6RL
Tel: 01864 505245

The South-East Falconry Group
Dean White
The Secretary
c/o Tilbury Community Centre
The Civic Square
Tilbury
Essex   RM18 8AA
Tel: 01489 896504

*enquire in writing

FALCONRY AND BREEDING COURSES

Falconry courses

The British School of Falconry at Gleneagles
c/o Emma Ford
The Gleneagles Hotel
Perthshire   PH3 1NF
Tel: 01764 62231
Fax: 01764 62134

Eagle-Owl Falconry
c/o Lee William Harris
Bridgend
Church View
Boston
Lincolnshire   PE22 0LE
Tel: 07798 906280
e-mail: leewilliamharris@hotmail.com

Breeding courses

Eagle-Owl Falconry
c/o Lee William Harris
Bridgend
Church View
Boston
Lincolnshire   PE22 0LE
Tel: 07798 906280
e-mail: leewilliamharris@hotmail.com

APPENDIX V

EQUIPMENT SUPPLIERS
AND BIRD OF PREY CENTRES

Equipment Suppliers

Eagle-Owl Falconry
c/o Lee William Harris
Bridgend
Church View
Boston
Lincolnshire   PE22 0LE
Tel: 07798 906280
e-mail: leewilliamharris@hotmail.com

Bird of Prey Centres

The National Birds of Prey Centre
c/o Jemima Parry-Jones
Newent
Gloucestershire   GL18 1JJ
Tel: 01531 820286

The New Forest Owl Sanctuary
Crow Lane
Ringwood
Hampshire   BH24 1EA
Tel: 01425 476487

BREEDERS OF HARRIS HAWKS AND OTHER BIRDS OF PREY

Paul Harris
210 Belswains Lane
Hemel Hempstead
Herts   HP3 9XB
Tel: 01442 399331

Lee William Harris
Bridgend
Church View
Boston
Lincolnshire   PE22 0LE
Tel: 07798 906280
e-mail: leewilliamharris@hotmail.com

The National Birds of Prey Centre
c/o Jemima Parry-Jones
Newent
Gloucestershire   GL18 1JJ
Tel: 01531 820286

VETERINARY SURGEONS WITH A SPECIAL INTEREST IN BIRDS OF PREY

The Clockhouse Veterinary Hospital
Wallbridge Road
Stroud
Gloucestershire   GL5 3JD
Tel: 01453 752555

A. G. Greenwood, MA, Vet. MB, FIBiol, MRCVS
J. Storm MRCVS
International Zoo Veterinary Group
Keighley Business Centre
South Street
Keighley
West Yorkshire   BD21 1AG
Tel: 01535 692000
Fax: 01535 690433

M. P. C. Lawton, B.Vet.Med; Cert.VOphthal; Cert.LAS; C.Biol; MIBiol; FRCVS
12 Fitzillian Avenue
Harold Wood
Romford
Essex   RM3 OQS
Tel: 01708 384444

M. H. Williams, BVSc, MRCVS
The Stocks Veterinary Centre
11 New Street
Upton-Upon-Severn
Worcestershire   WR8 OHP
Tel: 01684 592606

OTHER ADDRESSES

Cage and Aviary Birds
IPC Magazines
Blue Fin Building
110 Southwark Street
London SE1 0SU
Tel: 020 31484171
e-mail: birds@ipcmedia.com

The Countryside Alliance
The Old Town Hall
367 Kennington Road
London   SE11 4PT
Tel: 0207 840 9200

The Department of the Environment,
Transport and the Regions
c/o Clive Rowlinson
Ashdown House
123 Victoria Street
London SW1E 6DE
Tel: 01712 764610

Exotic Direct (Bird Insurance)
Bocks Braithwaite (Sussex) Ltd
4 Bridge Road Business Park
Haywards Heath
West Sussex RH16 1TX
Tel: 01444 412118

The Falconers & Raptor Conservation Magazine
PW Publishing Ltd
Arrowsmith Court
Station Approach
Broadstone
Dorset   BH18 8PA
Tel: 01202 659910

The Independent Bird Register
Tiercel House
Falcon Close
Scotten
North Yorkshire
Tel 01748 830112

IBR Falconer's Directory
Tiercel House
Falcon Close
Scotten
North Yorkshire
Tel 01748 830112

INDEX